Aurea Vidyā Collection*

——— 19 ———

* For a complete list of itles see page 133.

This book was originally published in Italian as *Il Sentiero della Non-dualità* (*Advaitavāda*) by Associazione Ecoculturale Parmenides (formerly Edizioni Āśram Vidyā), Rome, Italy

First Published in English in 2016 by
Aurea Vidyā
39 West 88th Street
New York, NY 10024

ISBN 978-1-931406-21-5

Library of Congress Control Number 2016906618

On the cover:
Gate of the Odeon in the ancient city of Ephesos

RAPHAEL

(Āśram Vidyā Order)

THE PATHWAY OF NON-DUALITY

(ADVAITAVĀDA)

AUREA VIDYĀ

‘The unreal cannot have the unreal as its cause, nor can the real have the real as its cause, nor can the real have the unreal as its cause, nor, [finally], can the unreal have the real as its cause.’

Gauḍapāda

CONTENTS

FOREWORD

This work, which we are offering in particular to the attention of those who are 'Lovers of Wisdom' (Philosophers), comprises a series of 'dialogues' with Raphael concerning some essential aspects of Non-duality.

Raphael is a seeker, a philosopher who has realized *Asparśavāda*, 'the path without support or relationship', keeping alive that *Advaita* tradition whose most representative 'restorers', from the two perspectives of realization and teaching, were Gauḍapāda and Śaṅkarācārya. In their written work, these two codified the fundamental principles of *Asparśavāda* (*Ajātivāda*) and of *Advaita Vedānta*.

Gauḍapāda's *Ajāti* (non-generation) and Śaṅkarācārya's *Advaita* (non-duality) were the high points for Raphael, because in *Advaita Vedānta*., and subsequently in Orphism, Platonism, Neoplatonism, the Cabala, and Hermeticism, he rediscovered the metaphysical conclusions which he had already reached.

Even as a child, Raphael felt a yearning to embrace Being. So he undertook an unvarying regimen which slowly brought him within the reach of a 'spiritual influence'. Step by step, and with the removal of obstacles, his consciousness revealed itself as pure essence, devoid of superimpositions.

According to Raphael, Philosophy means complete knowledge and realization, where knowing, the known and the knower perfectly coincide. The true philospher, the 'lover of wisdom', is the one who realizes the harmony of thought and being which manifests in a particular lifestyle, so that the one who understands, knows how to be master not only of thought but also of life. He reflects the concept of the Greek and Eastern philosopher whose philosophy consisted primarily of self-revelation, an unveiling of the knowledge that has been pursued.

Meeting the Absolute, the 'Whole' (as Plato says), Being rather than becoming, involves a definite subsequent change in all one's normal points of view, in the very meaning of life, and provides a new scale of values. The knowledge of the Whole brings with it a 'release from chains', an 'ascent' and a 'conversion of the whole person', a change of life, or, as Raphael often says, a 'transformation of consciousness'.

In conclusion, we would like to point out that in these dialogues there is a consideration, a resolution of a topic which transcends geographical and ideological boundaries in such a way as to be of interest to the whole of humanity. The replies are given by Raphael in the light of the knowledge of *Advaita,* but with a conceptual terminology that is in harmony with the Western mind and its particular approach to philosophy.

Aurea Vidyā

NON-DUALISM, DUALISM, AND MONISM

Q.[1] What is the meaning of the following terms that are often used by *Vedānta*: dualism, monism, monotheism, and non-dualism?

A. Every philosophical or cosmological vision which affirms two opposing and mutually irreducible principles to explain the Real is a dualistic vision.

Philosophical dualism is an answer to the problem of Being, which is considered twofold, being made of matter and spirit, of ego and non-ego, eternally in opposition and independent of one another.

Religious dualism, on the other hand, posits two principles in eternal contraposition and antinomy. It explains the presence of evil in the world and the very existence of the world as the outcome of the constant struggle between two eternal principles, the one called Good, the other Evil. These two opposing principles are often personified as God and Satan: the former the expression of Good, the latter of Evil.

Every dualistic concept – whether philosophical or religious – recognizes, in other words, two distinct causes, or two independent *substances*, to use the words of Aristotle, which due to their very nature can never meet, never relate or resolve themselves. This implies

[1] Q = Question; A = Answer.

that – at the manifest level – all contradictions, all antinomies, which arise and exist, can never be resolved. Two parallel lines, however much they be drawn out to infinity, can never meet.

Evil, considered as an absolute Reality, just like Good, can never be overcome by Good, and vice versa.

Dualism presents from the outset contradictions that cannot be solved or supported.

Philosophical, religious or cosmological monism conceives the multiplicity of manifestations as the effect of a single *substance*. It is obviously opposed to both dualism and pluralism. According to pluralism, Reality is made not of two but of several *substances*.

Monism can be compared to the mathematical one from which all numbers derive. The multiplicity of numbers is simply the multiplication of the one.

There is the materialistic monism according to which only one *substance* exists; matter, and all other categories, including spirit and even consciousness, are the epiphenomena of the one material *substance*. And there is – in total opposition to the former theory – spiritualistic monism, for which all can be traced back to a single *substance*, which is the Spirit.

For monism every existing element – of any type and at any level whatsoever – is real, because it represents the emanation or multiplication of the sole Reality. From this standpoint we might say that monism is pantheistic. Thus, within the field of monism we have to include Spinoza's pantheism, which declares the oneness of *substance* and the identity of God and nature.

In realistic pantheism, although all antinomies, such as good and evil for example, go back to the original unity, they must be considered real and therefore they cannot – on the plane of manifestation – be resolved or transcended. Evil, ignorance, unhappiness, limit, etc., are universal realities about which nothing can be done by man, because they are consubstantial with the One. We can say that the One contains within Itself the dialectics of opposites. All manifested effects, polar or dual as they may be, are contained in the First Cause. This means, naturally, attributing good and evil themselves to the One Principle.

Q. What is monotheism?

A. Monotheism – typical of religion – affirms the existence of a single Divinity. It is therefore opposed to polytheism and fetishism.

Some religions admit of a number of gods to control the laws of the universe as second principles; however, as these gods are made to derive from a single supreme God who includes them all, these religions may be considered to be monotheistic.

Here too emerges the impossibility of overcoming consciential, psychological and formal dualism because this has emanated from, or has been created by, the same God.

If the world is Real, then it is not possible to change, transform or redeem it. It will never be possible to rectify or redeem what really *is*.

Q. What is non-dualism, then?

A. Non-dualism is neither monism nor monotheism and, of course, it is not dualism.

Since monism might be assimilated to the mathematical one and the latter to multiplicity, to avoid misunderstandings the term 'non-dual' is used. In other words, the unity that is not multipliable, which does not generate or is not mathematical is called non-dual. This non-dual unity may be considered to be of a metaphysical order.

From the mathematical one, which is the generating principle of the total series of numbers, we arrive at the metaphysical One which is beyond all possible numerical nomenclature.

If according to monism and dualism the universe or object is created by or emanates from the First Cause, according to non-dualism the universe or object is neither creation nor emanation, but a simple phenomenon of *māyā*[1] projected upon the universal or individual screen by the projecting power of what we call mind. Thus, for example, our dreams or ideations – whether sleeping or waking – are simply projections or *māyā* that have no absolute reality and therefore may dissolve at any moment. The universe is a continuum and discontinuum that can be resolved and transcended. It is not, therefore, a creation – in the sense generally given to this term – because the Supreme Reality, being complete in itself, does not *need* to create, nor is it an emanation because the Supreme Reality does not exhaust itself in the manifest, nor does it transform itself to become other than what it is.

An individual, planetary or cosmic form or body is the effect of a movement which, were it to cease, the form would disappear.

The universe is a 'dream' (but this term must not be taken literally). We have a *body* and we are *moving*, because we are dreaming. If we wish to emerge from all apparent consciential, psychological and formal dualism, we must *wake up* and stop the movement. It is not Reality in itself that moves, it is not Reality in itself

[1] See the chapter entitled '*Māyā*'.

that causes dualism, but it is the 'movement' of the *jīva* (the living soul) which in turn is a *projection* or *reflection* of the absolute Self. Thus when we are in a train, because of *māyā* it seems to us that the landscape outside is moving, while in reality it is the train. From this point of view, the mathematical one and dualism are not absolute realities according to non-dualism, they are not *substances* but *appearances* and as such they can be transcended and resolved. 'Evil', and this applies also to 'good', is not a reality in itself: it is not *substance* but *appearance*, a particular *movement* that can be resolved and transcended. The universe of names and forms is not *ipseity*: it is not a reality which lives by its own life. It is not Being, but is simply movement (apparent if seen from the point of view of the absolute Reality) which causes non-substantial events or things. Our nightly dreams are not absolute realities, are not eternal, are not *substantial*, have no origin and nowhere to go: they are only phenomena projected by the mind upon the immobile screen of our being. To say that a dream *is* the individual himself or that the individual *exhausts* himself in the dream, or again, that the dream is eternal and immortal is pushing things too far. What causes this vital 'appearance', these worlds – apparently solid and immortal – is *māyā*.

Between the Real and the unreal (which appears real) stands *māyā*. It is sufficient to eliminate *māyā* to discover a single *substance*, that is, the Supreme Reality which is always identical to Itself.

Q. But can *māyā* be studied empirically and consciously?

A. When we want to study our dreams consciously, an unexpected event occurs: we awaken and wakefulness dispels our dream as if by magic. The ego and the non-ego of the dream (duality) disappear.

When we wish to examine empirically the snake we have seen instead of a rope, the snake disappears and we are left with the rope.

When we try to examine *māyā* consciously, it disappears, taking with it all dualism and antinomy, and in its place we find Being, Reality and the Absolute Constant. *Māyā* cannot be observed or analyzed empirically because it is not a reality.[1] Wanting to see or trace *māyā* is like looking in the air for the footprints of a bird, says Śaṅkara. Though not seen, *māyā* can be resolved and transcended by means of *vidyā*, metaphysical Knowledge.

We adhere to things because we believe them to be real and true, capable of granting satisfaction and fulfilment. In so doing we become alienated, as our completeness and happiness is dependent on something other than ourselves. But the 'other' is a mere mirage, a non-substance unable, through its particular nature, to grant us *summa pax*. According to non-duality, the error is believing in things that ultimately are not. In order to eliminate this error, the result of *avidyā* or erroneous knowledge (opinion or *doxa*), we need *vidyā* or noetic knowledge.

Q. Can we say, then, that the world of names and forms can be transcended and resolved by the power of Knowledge (*vidyā*)?

---

[1] Śaṅkara, *Vivekacūḍāmaṇī* (The Crest-Jewel of Discernment): *ślokas* 12 and 110. Translation from the Sanskrit and commentary by Raphael. Aurea Vidyā, New York.

A. As long as the 'snake' is seen and perpetuated by the projective power of the mind, it is considered as existing, real and substantial. It is only when we awaken and recognize the true being or rope that the snake disappears without leaving a trace. Thus, according to non-dualism, the world of names and forms is both real and unreal, depending upon the point of view from which it is observed and considered.

Q. Has the metaphysical One been seen and pointed out only by the Vedic Tradition?

A. The Vedic Tradition is only one branch of the One Tradition. The Tradition of the Sacred Mysteries of ancient Greece – above all the Orphic Tradition – recognized the metaphysical One, even though this truth was revealed only at the very last levels of the Great Mysteries.[1]

It is sufficient to go back to Plotinus, who took up and gave new life to the ancient Mystery Tradition. He says:

> '... It is necessary then that the One must be without form [That or *Turīya* of the *Vedānta* Tradition]. But if It is without form It is not essence; for essence must be something well determined, that is, defined [essence is the universal Spirit or the *saguṇa Brahman*, qualified and determined]; but it is impossible to apprehend the One as a particular thing: for then It would not be a *principle*, but only that particular

[1] For the harmony between certain aspects of Western philosophy and Eastern philosophy, the reader is referred to points 4, 5, and 6 of the 'Introduction to the *Upaniṣad* as presented by Raphael. Bompiani, Milan.

thing of which you say that it 'is this'. [In *Vedānta* 'this' corresponds to the manifested].

Now, if each determination is only within that which *becomes*, to which of these determinations will you resort in order to apply it to It? [Determinations and becoming belong to the world of appearances and not to that of pure Being]. Since It is none of these, all that can be said of It is that It is beyond them; but these things are realities and Being: consequently, It is beyond Being. [And in his desire to avoid doubts concerning the reality of the metaphysical One, Plotinus is careful to state:] In truth, 'beyond Being' does not express 'something determined' - which posits nothing in a positive way - and does not even express a name for It ['beyond name and form', as *Vedānta* has it], but conveys a purely negative idea: 'it is not this' [which corresponds exactly to the '*neti*, *neti*' of *Vedānta*: 'it is not this, it is not this'; 'this' is what Plotinus meant earlier by this term, that is, what is manifested].

But with such an approach the One is never encompassed; in any case, attempting to encompass that which is naturally infinite is a ridiculous undertaking; anyone claiming to do so would block the very way that he is following.

Conversely, just as anyone wishing to contemplate the being of Spirit should not have within himself any image of the sensible world, if he is to attain the vision of what is beyond the sensible [these words clearly indicate that the *Ātmā* or Spirit cannot be known through the senses or by means of the empirical mind, for *Ātmā* or Spirit is beyond the sensible].

Again, anyone wishing to have the vision of what is beyond Spirit itself as an object must jettison everything that is within Spirit in order to see: and clearly it is by means of Spirit [through the intuition of *noûs* or suprasensible intuition] that he can grasp that It exists; but how It exists he can grasp only by jettisoning the contents of Spirit [but to understand its Reality it is necessary to set aside even the functions of Spirit, because the One is known through an act of Identity].
[...] However, we human beings are convulsed, as if by birth-pangs, in our uncertainty concerning the words that should be uttered and we speak of the Ineffable and we hazard names, in our eagerness to signify It to ourselves as best we may. ['Words turn back, together with the mind, being incapable of knowing the *Brahman*.' *Taittirīya Upaniṣad*: II, 4].

'But It is without form, that is, it is devoid even of a spiritual form [...] therefore It is not "something", neither quality [unqualified and thus *nirguṇa*], nor quantity [beyond space and thus beyond time], nor Spirit [because It is beyond Being itself or *saguṇa Brahman*], nor Soul. It is not even in movement and, on the other hand, It is not at rest [because It is beyond all relationship]. It is not in space and It is not in time. Instead, It is the single Ideal, completely enclosed within Itself [*Brahman* is alone and without a second, absolute Silence, as the *Upaniṣads* say] or rather, It is the Formless which exists prior to every ideal, prior to movement, prior to stillness, because these values pertain to being and make it multiple [every correlation and duality participates in the mathematical One and not in the metaphysical One].

[...] Look! It must be posited as a unity whose reach is much greater than that which is the basis of numerical unity or the geometric point.
[...] Yet It should be conceived as infinite, not because It is endless either in size or in number, but because Its power is not circumscribed. Of course, whenever you think of It as Spirit or God, It is always more [and hence It is beyond Being or God with qualifications or *saguṇa Brahman*].'[1]

[1] Plotinus: *Enneads* V, 5, VI; VI, 9, III and VI. By V. Cilento. Laterza, Bari. Cf. also Raphael's 'Foreword' to Giuseppe Faggin's edition of Plotinus.

REAL AND UNREAL

Q. What is meant by real and unreal in Śaṅkara's *Advaita* and Gauḍapāda's *Asparśavāda*?

A. The problem of real and unreal, of Being and non-being, is very complex; therefore one gets different answers depending on the perspective from which one looks at the question. Thus we are obliged to illustrate this subject with an example.

Let us take a form or body, such as a cloud in the sky: is it real or unreal? Is a dream real or unreal?

Some hold that it is real, others that it is not, and others still that it is both real and unreal (*sat-asat*). It all depends upon one's point of view, on one's own position of consciousness or the particular system of co-ordinates which one is using to analyze things.[1]

Those who hold that a cloud in the sky – by way of example – is real, trust in a knowledge of an empirical, perceptive and sensory kind, the kind of knowledge based on the five senses. If sight sees, touch touches, taste tastes, it cannot be said, they maintain, that what we see, touch and taste is unreal or an illusion. What can

[1] For a fuller understanding of these aspects, see the chapters 'What is intended by Reality' and 'Threefold Knowledge' in Raphael's *Tat tvam asi*. Aurea Vidyā, New York.

be touched and seen is there, it occupies space, it lasts in time and can be observed and experienced by all.

Those who hold that 'things' do not exist conceive reality as non-sensory, non-material and non-substantial. According to them – consider pure idealism and acosmism – ontological reality is exclusively ideal. 'Things' have no reality of their own and the Spirit or Being cannot be the object of sensory knowledge, because it is beyond the senses. Therefore pure Being exists, while all that is not Being is unreality.

Those who maintain that things are real and unreal (*sat-asat*) – synthesizing the other two points of view – have a particular conception of reality which must be examined because it is not as superficial and reductive as the first two concepts.

Let us briefly see what kind of reasoning lies behind this third point of view.

If our senses see, touch and perceive, we obviously cannot say that we touch and see 'nothing'. Nothing – like the horns of a hare or a barren woman's child – can be perceived, touched or seen by any of the senses, however perfect they may be. Therefore we cannot support the thesis of those who hold that the senses perceive 'nothing' or that things do not exist.[1] However, at this stage we must go further into the problem and make a number of points.

To think that nothing exists beyond objectivity because the senses or figurative thinking cannot perceive it means either being absolutist or one-sided or else it means refusing to investigate and to find a solution to the problem. Things – a cloud in the sky – *appear* and *disappear*, they are and they are not, they

---

[1] Cf. *Māṇḍūkyakārikā*, by Raphael, III.28. AureaVidyā, New York.

come and they go, they are born and they die. In other words, they change continually. The senses themselves that touch and see soon cease to touch and see because the datum disappears.

On the other hand, it is legitimate to ask: what do our eyes really see? What our retina perceives as an image is a series of luminous vibrations which come from things outside us. When our senses see or touch things, they are not seeing and touching the things *in themselves* but rather their images given to the retina or to the tactile organs by their vibrations. The mind – as the sixth sense – translates and interprets the images obtained by the retina but not the thing *in itself.* Our truth springs from the interpretation or translation of a 'sensory image.'[1]

Besides – as we have already mentioned – the vibrations caused by things are not constant, are not absolute, because they are subject to endless modifications and the image we perceive, as a result, is altered too. Matter undergoes continuous change, it is a force-field and therefore it is impossible to grasp the thing in itself or the *ipseity* of matter.

From this point of view then, a cloud in the sky is certainly perceived, but a moment later one must admit that it is no longer perceived. This is a matter of fact, this is evident. It is an empirical fact of experience. Therefore, how can we say that things are real and absolute? A true and genuine reality must be always seen, perceived and found, within and outside time, and in every place. If this so-called reality appears to our senses

---

[1] Cf. the first verses of the *Dṛgdṛśyaviveka*, a philosophical investigation into the nature of the Seer and the seen, by Raphael. Aurea Vidyā, New York.

and then disappears like a flash of lightning or a mirage in the desert, to what extent can we say that it is real?

To consider as real or absolute what appears and disappears inevitably means wanting to force matters. On the other hand, the empiricists do not accept dreams as real, and yet dreams are perceived by the senses just like any other datum.

We are mistaken when we say we know things, because – as we have said above – we only know the *image* we have of things. And we know that even this image is subject to alteration and change in time and space.

Reality, fragmented into indefinable and fleeting phenomena, does not guarantee the stability and certainty of knowledge, but leaves it a prey to gnawing relativism, incapable of determination. Thought dies in anguish, losing itself in frustrating aporias and contradictions.

We must also say that the empiricists recognize all this, but as they do not wish to arrive at the point reached by the pure idealists, and as they are attached to their own point of view, they are obliged to make the following paradoxical statement: Reality is appearance, relativity, and change. But this statement does not agree with reason, if only for the simple fact that if everything is relative and changing then even the statement 'All is relative' is relative.

If a being is relative and inconstant, how can it portray an absolute reality or a reality of any other order and dimension? In other words, a relative being can speak only of relative truths. Thus, what the empiricist sees and touches is not Reality with a capital R, but a simple phenomenon which appears and disappears. However, a phenomenon is not a pure nothing: it is the effect of a particular movement which determines the appearance of a form or body, of an event that is not 'substance'. This movement, in turn, is an effect because its existence is the outcome of a relationship.

If the empiricist is obliged to consider all as relative and impermanent, then his idea coincides, in part, with the *Advaita* point of view, that is, with a point of view which is apparently the very opposite of his own. Opposites meet when one tries to really understand them.

Now, let us examine the point of view considered before which states that only Being, and not becoming, exists.

When examining the empirical view, we stated that it is impossible to reject the object altogether; however, we concluded that what we know is not reality but phenomenon or becoming or the mental and individual *interpretation* of such a phenomenon.

And if all we see and touch is phenomenon or movement, there must be a datum upon which such a phenomenon or movement depends. It is not possible to see phenomena or effects which do not depend upon causes or principles. Since becoming is *abaliety*, it cannot depend upon itself.

How can we know the Being that lies behind the phenomenon and behind mental and sensory interpretation, that being which the empiricists would like to touch and see as if it were a phenomenon or object?

If a phenomenal *object* can be seen and touched with equally relative, phenomenal and objectual tools, Being as pure *Subject* can only be known through Being, through an act of deep awareness of oneself as Being or subject, since Being, as a matter of fact, is not an 'object'.[1]

When we eliminate or transcend the becoming or phenomenon, Being reveals Itself in its absolute reality and *aseity*.

If the relative can be known by putting oneself upon the plane of relativity and upon that of simple interpretation, Being can be known by putting oneself upon the plane of *identity*. Western philosophy, in general, has not solved the problem of the knowledge of Being, because it has always put itself upon a dualistic plane, even while believing that it is stating the Oneness of reality.

Q. Can Being be experienced?

A. Being can be experienced only on the plane of identity. Thus traditional Philosophy, or Philosophy which leads to realization, proposes the knowledge of Being through the *realization* of Being.

Q. So does *Advaita* embrace both the Philosophy of Being and that of becoming?

A. Yes, because it includes three levels or stages of Reality (*satya*) in its view:

- *pāramārthika* = supreme or absolute Reality;
- *vyāvahārika* = empirical or phenomenal reality;
- *pratibhāsika* = illusory or apparent reality.

---

[1] For a deeper understanding, cf. *Dṛgdṛśyaviveka*, op. cit. and chapter XIII of the *Bhagavadgītā*, by Raphael. Aurea Vidyā, New York.

Pāramārthika is that Reality which cannot be contradicted by any other reality or existential experience, because there is no 'second' to which it can relate.

Vyāvahārika is the empirical reality which the five senses see and know. This is the phenomenal reality which is perceived in the world of names and forms and which can be contradicted by other realities and experiences.

Pratibhāsika is illusion, like the illusion we have when we see a mirage or two moons instead of one.

Asat, non-being in the strictest sense, is the non-existent, the unreal, like the hare's horns and the barren woman's child.

But compared with *pāramārthika* Reality, one may say that even *vyāvahārika* truth, the empirical truth, is illusory because it is impermanent and inconstant.

Thus the ultimate conclusion of *Advaita* is that Being and becoming are both dialectical 'moments' of the Absolute or non-qualified supreme Reality (*nirguṇa*).

AJĀTIVĀDA AND ASPARŚAVĀDA

Q. Gauḍapāda, in his *Māṇḍūkyakārikā,* speaks of *Ajātivāda* and *Asparśavāda*. But what are *Ajātivāda* and *Asparśavāda*?

A. In order to understand this metaphysical vision, one must first of all understand the philosophical attitude of *Vedānta* in general.

In the Hindu Tradition there are six *darśanas* connected to the *Vedas*. In contrast to Western philosophical systems, which are the outcome of mere individual speculations by isolated philosophers using *manas* or mind, these *darśanas* represent points of view, visions, or perspectives regarding the Vedic teaching.[1] It must also be kept in mind that in the East, philosophy and religion – in their purest sense – are united; philosophy is a way of being, a matter of consciousness, and not merely a mental approach. In other words, philosophy implies realization: *to know is to be*. Therefore when we speak of philosophy and metaphysics we understand them in their purest traditional sense. We could also speak of the philosophy and metaphysics of realization, such as we find, for example, in Pythagoras, Plato, and Plotinus, because they involve

[1] For a deeper understanding, see S. Radhakrishnan, *Indian Philosophy*, vol. II, 'The six Brahmanical systems'. George Allen & Unwin Ltd., London 1962.

the *very consciousness* of the being and not merely the mind as a simple discursive factor.

In order to grasp the Real, these *darśanas*, being points of view or perspectives of consciousness, start from certain *perspectives* that may be more or less complete, inclusive, and universal. Thus, for example, the *Sāṁkhya darśana* (*sāṁkhya* means 'enumeration') starts from the empirical rather than from the metaphysical outlook; it counts all the modifications that substance undergoes, from primordial matter (*prakṛti*) – under the impulse of *puruṣa* – to gross physical matter. This is undoubtedly a valid point of view, but it considers becoming rather than Being. We must point out, however, that it is not a materialistic *darśanas*, because the aim of *Sāṁkhya* is to free the *puruṣa* from the modifications of *prakṛti*.[1] *Puruṣa* corresponds approximately to essence or spirit as conceived in Western philosophy, and *prakṛti* corresponds to substance or matter. We may say, however, that it is a dualistic point of view in that it presents the two poles, *puruṣa* and *prakṛti*, as co-eternal. This does not mean that it is opposed to monism, but merely that Kapila, the compiler of *Sāṁkhya*, begins his treatise on the One when it is already differentiated or polarized. For example, we can study dense, physical matter from the molecular, the atomic, or the sub-atomic point of view. It is obvious that, according to the branch of studies, the point of view changes, although there is no contradiction between one viewpoint and any others.

---

[1] Cf. Īśvarakrṣṇa, *Sāṁkhyakārikā*, 62. By Corrado Pensa. Associazione Ecoclturale Parmenides, Roma. *Kārikā* 62 reads, 'No soul is bound or liberated, nor does it transmigrate. It is nature (*prakṛti*) alone, with its numerous stages, that is bound or liberated or undergoes transmigration.'

If, therefore, we grasp the fact that the *darśanas* are points of view, we realize that the various authors, the compilers of the *darśanas*, 'saw' Reality from different consciential viewpoints, which are the states of consciousness they reached, the positions they realized. Gauḍapāda – to use the analogy mentioned before – goes beyond the substantial texture, beyond the molecular condition, beyond the atomic state, to touch upon the state of elementary essence which is beyond all manifested factors. It is obvious, therefore, that Gauḍapāda (the compiler of the *Ajātivāda*) and Kapila (the compiler of the *Sāṁkhyavāda*), starting from different standpoints, arrive at different conclusions which are not opposed to each other or mutually exclusive. We should emphasize, however, (by analogy) that the molecular point of view, compared with the elementary one, is characterized by its relativity and non-absoluteness. The molecules are *born*, they *develop* and *disappear*, while the elementary state *subsists*. And indeed, the molecules dissolve into the elementary state because they are not absolute or constant. Mass (a body or a compound) dissolves into energy. From this point of view, and by transposing the whole onto a metaphysical level, *Ajātivāda* presents the characteristic of absoluteness and universality as compared with *Sāṁkhyavāda* which, however valid, is nonetheless reductive.

Q. Then did Gauḍapāda 'see' Reality in its ultimate non-determination?

A. Yes, he did. Gauḍapāda, by adopting the perspective of the Absolute as such, or of pure Being (*advaita*), was able to say, rightly, that in It there is no birth or generation or modification.[1] Pure Being was never born,

[1] *Māṇḍūkyakārikā*, II, 32 and IV, 57, op.cit.

and so It cannot die or cease to be. And if It is not born there can be no real manifestation. If the Absolute Being cannot transform Itself or become multiple, then, Gauḍapāda asks, what is it that we see? This is the wonderful metaphysical or *advaita* perspective of Gauḍapāda's *Ajātivāda*.

To continue the analogy, the atom on the gross, physical level is the first determination from which the various physical compounds arise, but beyond the atom there is no form or body: there is only 'formless' energy. In other words, there is no manifestation as we know it. Gauḍapāda, by moving to the metaphysical level, went beyond the first Determination or Being from which the formal universes arise, but beyond the first Determination there is no universe, no form, no compound, either atomic or molecular. We can say that beyond the first Determination there is the unqualified (*nirguṇa*), undetermined state.

Ajātivāda, seen from the perspective of the manifest – and the manifest includes the gross or physical, the subtle, and the causal or germinal states –, might seem a logical absurdity and a pragmatic impossibility, but this is understandable. Identification and assimilation with one state of consciousness excludes the understanding of another state. If the individual, for example, identifies with form or becoming (dualism in general), he will never be able to understand a point of view that goes beyond duality. If the individual identifies with his physical body (substance), he will never be able to understand himself in terms of pure Being that is never born, never grows and is never caused. A metaphysical 'Vision' implies going beyond the perspective of space, time, and causality; space, time, and cause are *determinations* inherent in forms, compounds, and phenomena. The more the consciousness identifies with the formal aspect, the greater will be the difficulty of going beyond this perspective.

Q. Gauḍapāda also spoke of *Asparśavāda*. What is this?

A. In the final analysis, *Ajātivāda* and *Asparśavāda* are one and the same thing. *Ajāti* means non-generation or non-birth and jāti means birth, generation, understood as the passage from Non-Being to Being. *Asparśa* is the path which leads to the ungenerated state of pure Being. Besides, sparśa means contact or relationship and *a-sparśa* means non-contact or non-relationship. Now the Absolute Being is often considered as having no relationship or contact with anything because, being one without a second (*advaita*), with whom or what could it establish a relationship or contact?

Q. *Asparśavāda* is also called the path without supports. Why?

A. The support of the ego, which is relativity, is constituted by the formal or manifest aspect and by the qualities (*guṇas*) which the substance expresses. *Asparśa*, because of its metaphysical nature of *vāda* or path, tends to remove all supports inherent in being. By eliminating all formal supports the reflection or ray of consciousness falls upon *That* which is pure Being without supports, relationships, or duality.

From a philosophical point of view we could say that *Asparśavāda* tends to eliminate the supports of time, space, and causality, which qualify the phenomenon, but not the noumenon.

Q. Is that why this path appears difficult?

A. Yes, because it is a metaphysics that leads to realization and tends to resolve all the determinations of Being. Since the ego is a manifested object, it fears its annihilation because it cannot imagine itself without form, time, or determination.

On the other hand, this is right; the molecular 'ego', to use an analogy, could never conceive itself as an atomic self because this belongs to another dimension.

Gauḍapāda in chapter III, *karika* 39, says:

> 'This *yoga* called '*asparśa-yoga*' (without contact), is, in truth, difficult for many *yogis* [aspirants] to comprehend, because they feel fear where there is no fear, and are afraid of it.'

And Śaṅkara, explaining this *kārikā,* declares that this metaphysical *yoga* is hardly accessible to *yogis* lacking in true knowledge. 'The *yogis*' says Śaṅkara 'are afraid (of this *yoga*) although they should not be; while practising this *yoga*, those who lack discrimination fear the extinction of their individuality, although (*asparśa*) is beyond all fear'.

And again, in *kārikā* 2, chapter IV, Gauḍapāda states:

> 'I pay homage to that *yoga* known as *asparśa* (without contact or relation), [source of] bliss for all beings, beneficial, free from disputation, and contradictions and taught [by the Scriptures themselves].'

Why free of contradictions? Because a contradiction or a disputation can be had only on the plane of duality. An empirical experience can be contradicted by another empirical experience; for example, the experience of waking by that of dreaming, that of dreaming by waking experience, and both are contradicted by deep dreamless sleep.

But in *Turīya* (the metaphysical state of pure Being) there can be no contradiction, because in it the experiencer and the experienced, or subject and object, do not exist.

Q. Thus from the point of view of the Absolute is nothing born?

A. From the point of view of the Absolute, there can be no birth or death, transformation or modification. From the point of view of the sun, earthly dawn and sunset are not absolute realities, and indeed they do not exist at all. There is no movement in the sun that can cause dawn and sunset (duality). There is no movement in pure Being that can cause birth and death.

Q. By what means did Gauḍapāda arrive at this truth?

A. By means of Knowledge, intuitive discernment and, naturally, by relying upon the authority of the *Śruti*.

Q. But what kind of knowledge?

A. *Vedānta* and Gauḍapāda propose various kinds of knowledge: one that is strictly illusory; one that is empirical and mediated, being presented by *manas* (projective mind) which knows only the object or form; and one that is immediate, the Knowledge of identity. In other words, one must distinguish between what is simple sensory opinion and what is true authentic Knowledge or Science, which reveals Reality, the Truth as it is.

Q. In short, then, what are the postulates upon which the Vision of *Ajātivāda* rests?

A. There is an unchanging, eternal, and actual Reality without generation or extinction, devoid of cause and effect, and of space and time, having no contradiction, One without a second.[1] And since Reality is constant and perfect unity, all that is differentiation, multiplicity, fleetingness and change cannot be the Ultimate and Supreme Reality but merely appearance, a representation which may seem to be real if observed from the point of view of opinion. Thus, the snake we see in place of the rope may be real as long as we believe it to be so, but at the touch of Higher Knowledge the snake proves to be a simple superimposition veiling the true identity of the rope.

The world of names and forms is nothing but mere appearance, a phenomenon which appears and disappears; it is a continuum and discontinuum which may be interrupted at any given moment when, that is, the Higher Knowledge of Identity (*paravidyā)* reveals itself within us. On the other hand, becoming offers a knowledge which is not, an unstable, uncertain knowledge; in other words, a non-knowledge. According to Gauḍapāda, all pairs of opposites, not being absolute, are resolved in the One without a Second.

---

[1] Cf. *Vivekacūḍāmaṇi*, *ślokas* 125, 465-470, op. cit.

PARMENIDES AND HIS VISION

Q. Which Western vision can we consider nearest to Gauḍapāda's *Ajātivāda*?

A. That of Parmenides. For Him, too, the teaching is based upon the above-mentioned postulates.

According to the Eleatic, there is only one Way (ὁδός) which solves the existential enigma, a way which 'is far from the way travelled by men', a pathway which leads to that door which transcends Day and Night (duality), which reveals the non-spatial Reality, a way which is '...without end (ἀτέλεστον).' Parmenides' Way is also the one which Yājñavalkya describes in the *Bṛhadāraṇyaka Upaniṣad* (IV, IV, 8):

> 'I have found the long, narrow, ancient way, and I have traversed it.
> By following it, the wise knowers of *Brahman* travel from this world *(loka)* to the celestial world once they are liberated.'

There is no doubt that the ὁδός of Parmenides is an initiatory path and the most modern and perceptive exegesis seems directed towards this conclusion.

Jaeger too agrees with this thesis when he writes: 'When facing this superhuman prelude [speaking of Parmenides' proem], no one would believe that the philosopher wished to put himself in the limelight. The vision of this mysterious event in the kingdom of light is an authentic religious experience: the experience of weak human eyes which turn towards the hidden truth, so that the whole of life is transfigured.' But this kind of religiousness 'must be sought in the religiousness of the Initiations and of the Mysteries. Parmenides was able to grasp this because in Southern Italy, in his day, these ideas were widespread.'[1]

According to the Eleatic, there exists, therefore, a single Way and a single Reality: Being, in that it is. It is unity, actuality, permanent, not subject either to birth or to death, all one and indivisible. Only that Being which is and does not become, which is complete and identical to Itself, is necessarily a Reality which fills everything, being total fullness:

> '...that Being is non-born, incorruptible (ἀνώλεθρόν),
> in fact it is in its entirety whole (οὖλον), immobile and without end (ἀτέλεστον).
> Nor was it ever, nor will it be, since it is now all together one (ἕν),
> continuous (συνεχές).
> Which birth for it, in fact, will you be looking for?
> How and from where is its birth?
> I will not allow you to speak or think of non-being
> because it is impossible
> to speak or think of
> what is not. What necessity would ever have pressed it to be born,
> earlier or later, if it derives from nothing?

---

[1] Werner Jaeger, *Die Theologie der frühen griechischen Denker*. Stuttgart, W. Kohlhammer, 1953.

It is thus necessary for it to be altogether, or not at all.
Never will the strength of true conviction grant that anything other than Being can be born from Being...'[1]

It can be known only through the mediation of that epistemological and noetic knowledge (νόησις: immediate understanding and, according to Stefanini's exegesis, 'contemplative ecstasy') which reveals only the supreme intelligible. Knowledge is that '...upon which Persuasion walks, and Persuasion is the follower of Truth'.[2]

For Parmenides, too, the world of names and forms (the empirical world) is mere appearance and is presented (as with Gauḍapāda) as a dialectical moment and not as absolute necessity:

'...This is why there will be only as many names as mortals
have established, in their conviction that
they are true:
coming to birth and perishing (ὄλλυσθαι), being and non-being,
changing position and undergoing mutation of luminous colour.'[3]

Becoming, contingency, and change seem to be and to exist from a false standpoint:

'Keep your mind far from this way of searching [the opinion which believes that things that are not are] ... This cosmic order, *apparent* as it is, I shall reveal to

---

[1] Parmenides, *On the Order of Nature, fr.* 8, by Raphael. Aurea Vidyā, New York.

[2] *Ibid, fr.* 2.

[2] *Ibid, fr.* 8, 38-40. Cf. *Chāndgya Upaniṣad*, VI, I, IV.

> you in detail, so that no opinion of any mortal may overcome you.'[1]

Aristotle in his *De Coelis* (1, 298 b, 14) states:

> 'Some of them [he is speaking of Parmenides and Melissus] denied the existence of generation and corruption altogether, saying in fact that nothing among the entities is either generated or dies, but it only seems so to us.'

That intellect which does not base itself upon Pure Being, unable to offer true Reality, projects and represents only names, simple words which lovers of learning – according to Plato – take for absolute, supreme truth. In this sense the following passage from Plato is illustrative:

> 'And would it not perhaps be an adequate defence, if we were to reply that he who truly loves knowledge should naturally tend towards Being, and refusing to be satisfied by the multiplicity of individual objects – *which are nothing but opinion* – should walk straight ahead without losing courage or diminishing his love before grasping the nature of each thing in itself with that part of his Soul whose activity is indeed to grasp the essence of things –for it has the same nature – and with this part of his Soul approaching and uniting himself with Being in Itself, generating understanding and truth, succeed in knowing in actuality, live a true life,

[1] *Ibid*, *fr.* 7 and 8.

> feed upon true nourishment, and thus cease suffering, but not till then, the pangs of childbirth?'[1]

We should furthermore point out that Parmenides – notwithstanding the different opinion of a number of exegetes – does not entirely negate the world of δόξα (the empirical world): he simply sets it in its proper place as 'appearance', as phenomenon, because it is resolved and transcended in the higher and supreme certainty of Being. The fact that the Goddess explains to Parmenides the structure and the workings of the world or δόξα means that this must have a degree of acknowledgement, because there can be no talk of nothing, of things that do not exist, such as the barren woman's child or the hare's horns, to use Gauḍapāda's and Śaṅkara's expressions.

> 'Nevertheless, you will also learn how the things that appear (δοκοῦντα) are to be evaluated by anyone who is making a thorough investigation of everything.'

On the other hand, Parmenides himself states that nothing can be said of non-being as such:

> 'It is impossible to declare or to think what is not.'

The Eleatic refutes only those who exchange the relative for the absolute, becoming (το μή ὄν) for Being (το ὄν), opinion (δόξα) for truth (αλήτεια). He also takes his stand against those who place Being and becoming upon the same plane.

Being is the metaphysical foundation of the 'world of names' or of becoming; and becoming, unable to justify itself, finds its justification in Being. Aristotle puts it as follows:

---

[1] Plato, *Politéia*, 490 b.

'Now, if nothing existed beyond individual things, the intelligible would not exist, for everything would be perceptible to the senses and as a result there would be no science, unless one is willing to state that sensory perception is science. Besides, there would be nothing eternal or motionless; but if nothing eternal existed, becoming itself would be impossible.'[1]

Thus the world of δόξα is the equivalent of appearance, similar to a dream when compared with the supreme Reality of Being which is its very foundation.

H. Schwabl writes:

'Men err only when they hold the apparent to be eternal and consider it as Being. ... On the other hand, they are right with regard to *doxa* when they acknowledge its uncertain and conditioned value.'[2]

'Thus, according to Schwabl, all pairs of opposites, such as Light and Night, 'may be unified in the higher unity of Being.'[3]

The things we see with our physical eyes are all *names* which appear and disappear and are annulled before the fullness and majesty of Being, which is and does not become.

We can say that this vision is in line with that of Gaudapāda and therefore with that of the *Upaniṣads*.

---

[1] Aristotle, *Metaphysics*, B, 4, 999 b.

[2] H. Schwabl, *Sein und Doxa bei Parmenides*, Wiener Studien. Bd. 66 (1953), *in Um Begriffswelt der Vosokratiker*, G.H. Gadamer (Darmstadt, 1968).

[3] *Ibid.*

Q. It seems, however, that Parmenides depicts Being as a sphere, while Gauḍapāda speaks of *Brahman* as infinite, bodiless and beyond categories which belong to manifestation.

A. This is right as far as Gauḍapāda is concerned, but to understand the teaching of Parmenides it is necessary to get into the spirit of his vision rather than dwell upon the face value of his words.

In ancient Greece the figure of the sphere was considered to be the symbol of perfection, of completeness, of unity, etc.; whereas all that was indefinite, formless, vague, indeterminate, nebulous, etc. was considered to be lacking in perfection and unity. Roundness gives us the impression of fullness, of self-sufficiency, of completeness as well as of harmony and beauty, and as completeness it transcends all categories and all temporal and spatial empirical determinations.

It stands for the pure metaphysical quality of the self-resplendent Being and its ideal circularity can extend itself as far as the infinite because it represents nothing less than the irradiation of the epicentre, the one, which is always identical to itself.

Thus, when one wished, for example, to speak of things in terms of perfection, unity, fullness, stability, etc., one referred to that standard of measurement that was represented by the sphere. Plato too – like the *Upaniṣads* – speaks of Being as a shining Sun. These are empirical images or analogies, the true value of which must be sought in the metaphysical dimension.

Parmenides speaks also of 'rounded truth':

'You must comprehend all:
the firm heart of the well-rounded Truth,

and the opinions of mortals in which there is no true certainty.'[1]

Now, were we to interpret literally the expression 'well-rounded truth' we would come up against a logical absurdity. But, if we enter into the spirit of Parmenides, of his day and of the Tradition, then everything will appear clear to us; 'spherical truth' gives us the idea of perfect truth, of perfect knowledge, of an indubitable truth of such stability that nobody may shake or destroy it, as against the truth of men which is instead mere opinion and therefore nebulous, vague, undefined truth and unstable knowledge.[2]

Here are a number of *kārikās* by Gauḍapāda which require no explanation:

> 'Hence I shall speak of That (*Brahman*), free of limitations, devoid of generation (*ajāti*) and always in a state of equilibrium. [Listen] how nothing is in any way born although it appears to be born.'
>
> '...and manifestation, expounded in many ways through the examples of clay, gold, sparks spraying everywhere, etc., is a didactic means (*upāyaḥ*) of enabling [the idea of unity] to be understood, but there is no distinction in any way.'

---

[1] *On the Order of Nature*, fr. 1, 29-30. 'well-rounded Truth': Truth is supreme and unchangeable, because philosophers consider the Centre and the sphere to be Limitless, like the Idea of perfection, the unchangeable centre-point from which comes the 'circumference', the movement. The nature of the sun and the planets is 'round'.

[2] Parmenides, *On the Order of Nature*, op. cit.

> 'The disputers affirm the birth of a non-born being. But how can what is non-born (*bhāvaḥ ajātaḥ*) and immortal become mortal?'
>
> 'The immortal cannot become mortal, nor can the mortal [become] immortal. A change of nature cannot happen in any way.'
>
> 'It is by virtue of *māyā* (*māyayā*), that this Non-born [*Ātman*] can differentiate itself and in no other way, because if differentiation were real, then the immortal would become mortal.'[1]

According to Parmenides, opinion (δόξα: representation, what appears to be true; sensory perception) is an erroneous vision of man 'where no truthful certainty abides', and which makes Being seem generated and multiple. According to Gauḍapāda it is *avidyā*, which can also be taken to mean sensory perception (simple projection, opinion, mental representation), which causes the appearance of things that are not.

> 'In truth, some seekers maintain the birth of what already exists, others [maintain] the birth of what does not exist, mutually opposing each other.'
>
> 'A datum which already exists cannot be reborn and a non-existing datum cannot come into existence....
>
> 'He, who believes that a being, immortal by nature, may become mortal, how can he [maintain at the same time] that the immortal, being born, may still preserve its immortal nature?

---

[1] Gauḍapāda, *Māṇḍūkyakārikā*, III, 2; 15; 20; 21; 19, op. cit

'The [true] nature [of a being] is that which is acquired forever, intrinsic, innate and not produced, that which does not lose its own [immutable] essence; this is how it must be understood.

'[The fourth chapter of the *kārikā* is about causation] A cause cannot be born from [an effect] which has no beginning; nor is an effect born in an autonomous way [from a beginningless cause], because a cause which does not exist [or which has no cause] does not, in truth, exist as a [causal] principle.

'The unreal cannot have the unreal as its cause, nor can the real have the real as its cause, nor can the real have the unreal as its cause, nor, [finally], can the unreal have the real as its cause.'[1]

[1] *Ibid*, IV, 3, 4, 8, 9, 23, 40.

ADVAITA VEDĀNTA

Q. We often hear people speak of *Advaita Vedānta* as a religion, a philosophy, and a metaphysics. But what is it really?

A. First of all we must underline the fact that certain questions are asked more in the West than in the East. In addition, the misunderstandings met with by many are compounded by the fact that some words have different meanings in the West and in the East.

It must also be pointed out that the answers given to the various questions are only intended to stimulate a deepening of the knowledge to be acquired through the reading of specific and suitable texts.[1]

In the West we have a concept of religion, philosophy and metaphysics that does not correspond to the Eastern meaning of the same terms. For us, the concept of religion is derived from the Judeo-Christian-Islamic context and has a precise meaning connected with the theological constructions elaborated by those religions. To speak of Hindu religion may seem improper, because Hinduism,

---

[1] In the notes to this book we refer the reader to various works for a deeper understanding of the topics expounded in these exchanges. It is also worth noting that the 'Aurea Vidyā Collection' contains many texts that are fundamental to the understanding of *Advaita Vedānta*.

on the whole, and over the ages, is a way of being, of living, of expressing oneself, rather than an organized, hierarchical and dogmatic religion in the Western sense. We may speak more appropriately of 'Hindu civilization', of 'Hindu consciousness', of 'Hindu attitude'.

Hinduism is based upon the *Vedas*, which, rather than a theological or dogmatic *corpus*, are a synthesis of philosophy, metaphysics, mysticism, cosmogony, traditional magic and other sciences, including those that are practical. The Hindu would say that in the *Vedas* there is all that one needs to know. The seeds of the upaniṣadic speculation and of the *Śāstras* are already present in the *Vedas*. The central ideas of Buddhism and of Jainism are not new: they too are present in the *Vedas*.

The Hindu holds that the *Vedas*, and therefore the *Vedānta*, that is, the later Scriptures that crown the *Vedas*, represent *Sanātanadharma*, the eternal *dharma* which is beyond time. This *dharma*, being timeless, has no history because it has no beginning. Judaism, Christianity, and Islam can all be dated, for they all have a precise beginning and a founder: Moses, Jesus, and Mohammed. Hinduism has no such founder. The *Ṛṣis* themselves, who drew up the *Vedas*, are only the transmitters of an eternal Truth which is non-human and beyond history. Many of the *Ṛṣis* are not even known by name; some of them have a name that is more mythical than real; for example, Vyāsa is held to be the compiler of the *Vedas*, of many other Vedic writings, and of the *Mahābhārata* itself, but Vyāsa refers to a 'function' rather than to the name of a person. It is a mythical name and cannot be considered in the same way as the name of Moses or Jesus.

In the West the concept of religion implies a founder (in space and time) who formulates certain moral and spiritual principles to be followed by the devotees. This is not so with Hinduism. Perhaps Buddhism is somewhat closer to this concept of religion, but even in this case many distinctions must be made.

Therefore Hinduism is not a religion in the Western sense; this is also why it is not easy to accept, be part of, or convert to Hinduism. A Jew who wishes to become a Christian has only to be baptized to become automatically part of the Christian religious community, but for any person who wishes to become a Hindu it is not a question of being baptized, and in any case no such baptism exists. Some hold that one must be born a Hindu, but it is also true that in the West there are many 'Hindu consciousnesses', just as in the East many feel Christians or Moslems. The term 'East' may be considered in a non-geographical sense. We should also note that in the East philosophy and religion always go together – the very opposite is true of the modern West. In the East the one complements the other. Gauḍapāda, for instance, commented on the *Māṇḍūkya Upaniṣad* from the standpoint of the *Śruti* and of *dialectical* philosophy. In other words, he united *Revelation* and philosophical reflection.

With reference to *Advaita Vedānta*, it is not really a question of speaking in terms of religion. *Advaita Vedānta* – whose codifier was Śaṅkarācārya – is obviously linked to the *Vedas* of which it has grasped its purely philosophical and metaphysical factors. Its roots are, therefore, Vedic, the trunk was nourished by Gauḍapāda – the Teacher of Śaṅkara's Teacher – and the branching tree with its abundant fruit was developed by Śaṅkara.

Advaita Vedānta may be considered as philosophy and metaphysics, but these terms are not to be taken in their Western sense.

In the West, especially in the modern West, philosophy is reserved to those who wish to demonstrate, through mental and discursive dialectic, *their* particular view of the world and of Being. In other words, they try to demonstrate truth by using discursive reasoning, but we know that mental discursiveness has its limits, because it can operate only on the plane of the contingent object. A rational and empirical 'demonstration' of Being, for example, implies setting oneself upon the plane of duality which, in turn, precludes not only the 'demonstration' itself but also the true *knowledge* of Being.

One may say that, in the West, philosophy suffers from the typically Western *consciential attitude* of looking at things from a dualistic, objectivist standpoint. It aims at knowing the external *object*, while Eastern thinking aims at knowing the *one* who wants to know the external object.[1]

Western philosophy is one of simple mental 'demonstration', whereas Eastern philosophy is one of *realization.* Besides, while the Western philosopher has produced a philosophical system of *his own*, often in contrast with and in opposition to the systems of other philosophers, the Eastern philosopher has not produced a system nor has he claimed ownership of his pronouncements.

Advaita Vedānta (like all other *darśanas*) is a *darśana* stemming from the *Vedas* and drawing from the *Vedas*, developing a 'perspective' or 'point of view' that already existed in germ in the *Vedas*. The word *darśana*, in fact, is not indicative of a closed philosophical system thought up by some solitary thinker or philosopher; its etymological meaning is 'to look', 'to observe'. It is a 'point of view' concerning the Vedic Scriptures, i.e.

---

[1] See the Preface by Raphael to Śaṅkara's *Vivekacūḍamaṇi*, op.cit.

Vedas and *Upaniṣads* (*Śruti*). But even Greek philosophy, in its precise meaning, was a philosophy which derived its content from the *Mysteries*. The *Mysteries* are a branch of that eternal Teaching which we have called *Sanātanadharma*. Orpheus, Pythagoras, Plato, Plotinus – to name but a few – all drew from the *Sacred Mysteries*.[1] And Christianity, while availing itself of the *Sacred Mysteries* (in the Mass, in fact, the statement 'Let us celebrate the Sacred Mysteries' is made) has refused and repudiated them. Thus, when we speak of philosophy we refer to that *Philosophia Perennis* which has no history and was not formulated by any human mind.

The term *metaphysics* has a more specific meaning and refers to that branch of philosophy which deals with the absolute Reality beyond all contingency, above the manifest in its integral extension, and therefore beyond time, space, and causality.

In the West of our own times, anyone who speaks of metaphysics may be burnt at the stake, so strong is the denial of the transcendent today. But, in truth, in the West of today philosophy no longer exists, because it has been reduced to the level of the philosophy of science, of politics, of law, etc.

---

[2] Cf. *Orphism and the Initiatory Tradition*, and *Initiation into the Philosophy of Plato*, by Raphael. Aurea Vidyā, New York.

METAPHYSICAL REALIZATION

Q. We often hear of realization of the Self, of the *ātman,* of the Spirit, etc., but what is meant by metaphysical realization?

A. First of all, let us see the etymological meaning of these terms or we may misunderstand each other.

What do we mean by realization? The verb 'to realize' means 'to make something become real', 'to translate into reality', 'to come true', 'to actuate', etc.

The meaning that is nearest to our case is 'to actuate'. To actuate means, in fact, 'to pass from power into act', to translate into *actuality* what is virtual.

The term 'actuate' implies, therefore, something that already exists. On the other hand, we could not actuate or translate into actuality what does not exist. Thus a child that grows actuates, realizes or manifests the physical and psychological potentialities that already exist in him or her. From this example we can understand that there is an *actuation* of even the psycho-physical qualities inherent in the individual. The majority of individuals do nothing but *realize* their own dreams, ideals, and projections, those qualities peculiar to their own psychological and physical self.

If being in its totality were just individuality, just empirical self, this kind of actuation would provide fulfilment and happiness. However, we know that this is not the case. Individuality is unhappy, dualistic, restless and dissatisfied; hence we have to admit that actuation by itself is not sufficient, or else it is a *false actuation.*

The empirical materialist tries to realize or actuate himself as an ego or individuality, but the world of the ego is full of conflict and pain, and egoistical and sensory happiness is so fleeting that it cannot even be tasted.

Fortunately there is another kind of realization or actuation, that inherent in the Self, in the true nature of the whole being, in the Spirit or *ātman*, in Being as such, in the divine part within us, if you wish to use more comprehensible terms.

This kind of realization is the actuation of our true Essence. And in the actuation of one's own Essence there cannot be conflict or bewilderment because it is a process which responds to the nature of the very same being: it is not something contrary to nature. To be is in the very nature of Being.

In individuation there is conflict and suffering because the emphasis is placed not on the being or Essence, but on the *false projection* that one has of oneself. From this point of view the term *realization* can be replaced by another one: *liberation*. Liberation from what? Liberation from the *false projection* that we are a separate, distinct and self-sufficient individuality, divided from our Essence or being, from our true 'I', which, to avoid confusion with the false I, we call Self-*Noûs*. Individuality does not actuate its true power, but only its own projections which it produces artificially and which, as a consequence, are forever changing. We – as individualities – pursue false ideals, false passions, false truths, so that in the non-actuation of our true power we experience conflict and are as if in blindness or ignorance (*avidyā*).

When, for instance, we see a snake instead of a rope – just to use the classical example – all our actions and behaviour are in line with the snake 'reality'. But, in so behaving, it is obvious that we come up against conflict due to the fact that the snake is not the effective reality: it is not the true power within us, which we need to actuate and manifest. It is just a false representation of the rope that we have conjured up. On the other hand, in order to be in harmony with true and authentic realization, we must actuate the rope, the *ātman*, the Self, which is the only absolute reality and which, in itself, is beyond all processes of power and act.

Q. So there is the liberty of the ego and the freedom from the ego, is there not?

A. Yes, the ego or snake, in order to be able to gratify its varied insatiable desires, needs to be without impediments and to feel free to actuate whatever it wishes. And this is impossible due to the very nature of existence; but even if we granted the ego every kind of liberty, it would still not be happy or fulfilled. Why? Because fulfilment is not in the nature of the ego, as this is only a false product or a false projection. What does not exist potentially cannot actuate or realize itself. Although the moon may wish to appropriate light from outside itself, it will never become a sun. The human physical body, though it may live for an incredible length of time, will never become immortal because one cannot 'become' immortal: one *is* immortal; and if one *is*, one does not seek immortality.

The empirical ego, since *it is not*, has to find its fulfilment, its raison d'être, and its realization, *outside itself*; and indeed it is obliged to, it is forced to. This means that at best it may find some kind of gratification, but a gratification that comes from other than itself cannot be permanent bliss or fulfilment. When one is dependent and under the sway of the law of necessity, there cannot be harmony, tranquillity, bliss, or fulfilment. If the empirical ego is searching, desiring, and longing, it means that *it is not* and every one of its realizations is a false realization, a false actuation.

Q. So metaphysical realization is needed, isn't it? What does this concept mean?

A. We have already spoken about realization, and now we need to understand the term *metaphysics.*

Originally the term *metaphysics* meant a series of texts which, on the basis of the order given to the works of Aristotle, came after the texts called Physics. The subject treated by Aristotle in that series of writings was called *Philosophia Prima.*

In time the term took on the meaning of 'beyond' matters belonging to the physical sphere, to become the 'science of the real in itself, seen as *beyond* immediate tangible appearance'.

From this point of view, metaphysics holds a higher position than the other fields of knowledge. Above all the various sciences of the *finite*, which deal with the partial, phenomenal and incomplete relations of being, there is the science of Reality in itself.

Metaphysics is the science of *aseity* (the property of a being which has in itself the cause and the end of its own existence), while physics is the science of *abaliety* (the property of a being which finds the cause of its existence in something other than itself).

We may add that physics deals with the relative or contingent, which depends on something other than itself, while metaphysics deals with what is or the Absolute, for it rests on itself, with itself, and by means of itself.

If we have understood the term *metaphysics*, then *metaphysical realization* means the actuation of the Absolute or of *aseity*.

Q. Can we go deeper into the concept of the Absolute?

A. According to the philosopher G. Zamboni, the term *Absolute* means: 'Etymologically, that which is *free from relationships*, or that which exists and is what it is, without any need to be related to anything else, or that which is fully sufficient, self-sufficient, independent of any other thing or reality. ... Therefore the Totality of the real, the Real as a whole, must be self-sufficient, fully independent, in order to exist or to be what it is. ... With the concept of being or entity or reality, the idea of totality is formed: *all that exists*, *all Reality*, *the whole of Reality*, outside of which there is nothing. The *whole of Reality* cannot depend on something else outside itself, because outside it there is nothing; thus the totality of what exists has in itself full sufficiency to exist and full independence. Either the *whole of Reality* is itself the Absolute and the Independent or else it contains them. In either case, the Absolute exists; one cannot doubt it; if anything, the existence of the insufficient and the dependent and its relation with the Absolute is less clear. But certainly, if there is something that exists, the Absolute exists.' (*Dizionario Filosofico*, Milan, 1978.)

Metaphysical realization, therefore, aims at the *actuation* of that which is 'free from relationships', that which has no need to be in relation to anything else', precisely because it is *aseity*. Let us see what Gauḍapāda says in his *kārikās* to the *Māṇḍūkya Upaniśad*:

> 'I pay homage to that yoga known as *asparśa* (without contact or relation), [source of] bliss for all beings, beneficial, free from disputation and contradictions, and taught [by the Scriptures themselves].'
>
> 'This *yoga*, called 'without contact' (*asparśa-yoga*), is, in truth, difficult for many yogis [aspirants] to comprehend, because they feel fear where there is no fear, and are afraid of it.[1]'

Śaṅkara comments: '*Asparśa* is the yoga without *sparśa,* having no contact or relation with anything at all; it is of the very nature of *Brahman* [Absolute]. Those who know *Brahman* call it by this name. In other words, *asparśayoga* is that which is free from all relationships. It becomes a blessing for all beings. ... We can say that the enjoyment of any particular type of object may bring happiness, but not constant well-being [we stated above that the happiness of the empirical ego is always contingent and fleeting because it is based on external factors]; this *yoga*, on the other hand, brings bliss and stable well-being at the same time, because its nature transcends the impermanent. In addition, it is devoid of oppositions. Why? Because it is devoid of contradictions [individuality is based on opposition, because it expresses itself at the level of ego and non-ego]. ... The idea is that this truth can be realized only in the wake of an impetus whose apex is awareness of the *ātman* as the sole Reality. ... In their practice of this yoga, those who lack discrimina-

[1] Gauḍapāda, *Māṇḍūkyakārikā*, IV, 2 and III, 39, op. cit.

tion fear the extinction of their individuality, although it (*asparśa*) is beyond all fear.

'Those who believe the mind and the sense organs to be a snake superimposed on the rope, and therefore to have no reality independent of *Brahman* actuate identity with *Brahman* without fear, enjoying in a natural way that eternal peace called emancipation, which depends on no other factor.'

Those who think that the psychological or empirical ego is their true reality undoubtedly fear metaphysical realization because they believe they will *extinguish*, *annihilate*, and lose themselves. And wanting at all costs to avoid the death of their ego – which is in any case perishable – they invent philosophies and sciences to support and satisfy their insecurity and incompleteness.

This philosophical view is typical of the present day where the mirage and the illusion of the 'golden calf' appears as the solution for the 'welfare' of the ego.

Q. So has *asparśa* realization no other aim than to *actuate oneself* in metaphysical Unity?

A. A dualistic philosophy cannot lead to the realization of metaphysical Unity. At most, it can realize the ontological One which already implies duality and which is not the Absolute.

On the other hand, true metaphysical realization implies actuating our most profound nature, which is Non-duality.[1] Now, our true nature (not that illusory 'second nature' represented by our empirical ego) is achieved by an act of Knowledge and of Identity.

[1] Cf. 'Realization according to Traditional Metaphysics' in *The Threefold Pathway of Fire*. Aurea Vidyā, New York.

To reveal our true nature we do not need any particular physical or mental 'exercises', though they may be used at the preparatory stages, but we have to eliminate the qualitative *superimpositions* that have been projected upon the Self or Being.

Q. Is metaphysical realization a question of knowledge, then?

A. This question helps to clarify further the concept of 'actuation' or of 'power' and 'act'.

Metaphysical Unity is pure actuation and excludes all movement from power into act: to speak of the eternally present and infinite Being in terms of even theoretical phases is impossible. The Ever-Present has no history, no actuation, no movement, because it has no birth (*ajāti*). Metaphysical realization, rather than being a question of actuation or realization as presented above, is an act of immediate Knowledge and awareness, because pure Being is not attained by steps or through supports, nor can pure Being be grasped in the process of actuation.

If we do not comprehend, by means of intellection, what we are and what we are not, we shall always remain in the sphere of sensory perception and of subject and object otherness.

Q. However, many kinds of yoga and religious teachings adopt empirical means rather than Knowledge.

A. Most people, through empirical means, 'actuate' *samādhis* which imply simple experimentation of individual states of consciousness, states outside the dense, gross sphere.

Individuality is not confined to the physical state, but extends also into the subtle, though substantial, state. However, in the subtle and even in the causal states (the three levels of existential manifestation) we are not in the realm of the Absolute or in the metaphysical sphere.

Pure Being is attained through Being, through a conscious awakening which resolves itself in Identity or in being Being.

THE THREE STATES OF BEING

Q. What do the three states of Being and the Fourth, mentioned in the *Māṇḍūkya Upaniṣad*, mean? There is also mention of the three worlds of manifestation; do these correspond to the three states? Some speak of seven worlds; is this perhaps in disagreement with the teaching of the *Upaniṣads*?

A. Every world can be subdivided into other worlds or spheres of existence; therefore mention is made of three, five, seven and even ten worlds. The number is of little importance, for it depends upon the point of view from which one wishes to examine things. For example, the physical plane may be taken as a whole or divided into its solid, liquid and gaseous dimensions; we know that within each of these there live and move entities which are different from one another. Thus in the 'liquid' dimension, although it belongs to the gross, physical domain, a world quite apart from the solid one lives and moves and may even be considered as a world unto itself with its own specific qualities. In any case, we can say with the *Upaniṣad*:

> 'All this is verily *Brahman*. This *ātman* is *Brahman* and the *ātman* has four feet or quarters (*pādas*).
> 'The first quarter (*pāda*) is *vaiśvānara*, whose sphere [of action] is the waking state...

'The second quarter is *taijasa*, whose sphere of action is the dream state...
'...the third quarter is *prājña*, whose sphere of activity is the state of deep sleep...
'It is invisible, non-acting... The Sages consider this to be the Fourth'.[1]

The *Māṇḍūkya* is defined as that *Upaniṣad* which alone synthesizes the whole of the *Vedānta* teaching.[2] We find in it the enunciation of the three states of Being as well as the Fourth which refers to the metaphysical and transcendent state.

All branches, both Western and Eastern, of the Tradition recognize the fact that the one Being expresses Itself, on the plane of manifestation, in different vital states, in different existential forms or in various modes. One may also say that Being expresses Itself in various vibratory states of consciousness, at both the formal and formless levels. It follows that we have to distinguish the existential plane from the entities that live and have their being on that plane. Let us take, as an instance, the dense physical plane, that on which we are experiencing our present lives: it is a plane of existence and is formed of solid, liquid and gaseous vibrations, etc., which belong to the gross plane of *vaiśvānara*. In all these vibratory states, as we have already mentioned, there are entities that live, move, and have their being. In the liquid state of the ocean there is an entire world, a way of being, millions of entities that express their qualities through

[1] *Māṇḍūkyakārikā,* II, III, IV, V and VII, by Raphael, op. cit.

[2] The *Muktikā Upaniṣad* (I, I, 26-29), where the existing 108 *Upaniṣads* are listed, states that the only *Māṇḍūkya Upaniṣad* is sufficient for *mokṣa* (liberation).

well-defined forms; in the gaseous state, or in the air, many more millions of entities carry on their existence and their being; and so on.

When the *Upaniṣad* speaks of *vaiśvānara* or *viśva*, it is referring to our bodily state, our physical being, our gross state, which corresponds to the gross universal plane of Being (*Virāṭ*). Thus we find that *viśva*, or the entity identified with viśva, has its experiences on a portion of the *Virāṭ* plane.

Viśva is the individual entity; *Virāṭ* is the universal Entity. And so *Virāṭ* is not only our planet: it is the totality of the worlds that express themselves at the gross level.

The sphere of action, of manifestation of the *jīva* or *viśva* (the soul embodied upon the gross plane) is that which man normally calls waking – compared to dream and sleep, of course. Through this state of consciousness and upon the existential plane of *Virāṭ*, the human *jīva* has various kinds of experience. This state is characterized by *ahaṁkāra* (the sense of ego), by *manas* (the empirical projective mind), by *kāma* (desire in its innumerable expressions) and by the gross physical body (*sthūlaśarīra* or *annamayakośa*, the body made of food).[1] Therefore the *jīva*, by means of appropriate *bodies* of manifestation, with their respective senses and faculties, experiences the *vaiśvānara* sphere.

---

[1] For a deeper understanding of sheaths or coverings, see the *Taittirīya Upaniṣad*, the *Bhagavadgītā*, and Śaṅkara's *Vivekacūḍāmaṇi*. Aurea Vidyā, New York. See also the word *Jīva* in the concluding notes to the *Upaniṣad* as presented by Raphael, op. cit.

But besides the dense physical plane, the being or *jīva* experiences with its subtle body (*liṅgaśarīra*) another existential plane, that of *Hiraṇyagarbha*.

Hiraṇyagarbha is a plane, a vibratory state or an existential condition even more extensive than the state of *Virāṭ*. We do not perceive it with our physical senses because these are capable of perceiving only the *Virāṭ* sphere. When the being or *jīva* leaves its gross body – through illness or for other reasons – it moves on to the state of *taijasa*, which is luminous: luminous because it illumines itself. In the same way, dreams are illumined by our own light.

The *taijasa* being with its vehicle made of more subtle and vibrating matter having, like the dense physical vehicle, *instruments* of contact – senses and faculties – experiences life inherent in the universal plane of *Hiraṇyagarbha*. During the physical embodiment, these senses and faculties belonging to the subtle body are dormant, although some are able to develop them, in which case we speak of extrasensory perception.

The sphere of *Hiraṇyagarbha* – like the sphere of *Virāṭ* – has many 'environmental levels' where the beings or *jīvas* with luminous bodies find opportunities of manifestation. Particularly on the subtle level, what guides the *jīva* towards one dimension or another is its vibratory state, its qualities, the energy which the *jīva* has inherited and modified in a certain way. Thus we speak of *Kāmaloka*, *Manavaloka* or *Hiraṇyaloka*. *Kāmaloka* (*loka*: place in the sense of state) is the 'environmental level' that is characterized by the quality of desire or feeling in all its expressive range. *Manavaloka* is the 'environmental level' that is characterized by the more creative, mental, ideal qualities, though still under the sway of *ahaṁkāra*, the sense of ego or the individualized state.

Hiraṇyaloka is the 'environmental level' that is characterized no longer by individualized qualities but by universal ones. It is the sphere of archetypes, or 'Ideas' which do not belong to the ego, whose sphere is *Manavaloka,* but to universal Being. The soul (*jīva*) on its true plane contemplates not its own ideal reflections, but Ideas. The noetic life is the fullness of the *act*, inasmuch as reflection of the *ātman* possesses the consciousness of *sat, cit, ānanda.*

Where do the highest expressions of genius come from? They come from the sphere of *Hiraṇyaloka.* One may say that the Soul has at last found its homeland, its place, its home. *Kāma* or desire and *manas* or empirical mind are no longer needed at the level of *Hiraṇyaloka*; the Soul *sees*, *contemplates* and immediately comprehends. Here, to see is to know (*veda* in Sanskrit derives from the root *vid* which means 'to see' or 'to know').

Kāma or desire, being an expression of lack and deprivation (not being and not possessing, one desires), has no further reason to exist, for the Soul, on its own plane, is.

In dreams everything comes from us; in dreams we are not in need of anything: we have merely to project all we desire within our particular sphere of existence.

But *Hiraṇyaloka*, *Manavaloka*, etc., are not dreams as such: they are equated to dream because they have similarities, but similarity *is* not identity.

> 'Such a life, unmoved and blissful, belongs to the gods, and evil cannot find a foothold anywhere there. If there is anything up there, it is certainly not evil,

but the first Good and the good of the second and third levels.'[1]

The world of bodies or *viśva* is a world of need, tension, and conflict, because it is essentially a world of privation, poverty, and non-being.

Prājña is the germinal, causal state, the state from which the determinations of manifestation arise; it is the geometrical point which, while having no dimension, is the origin of the line and the plane. It is the *noumenon*, the germ containing all the potentiality of being.

The being or *jīva-prājña* manifests itself upon the existential level of Being, of *Īśvara*; this is the *Brahmaloka* level, the abode of *Brahmā*, where multiplicity dissolves into unity. In it we can see how the three states are but one, having different modes of expression; in it there are no distinctions, there is no duality, there is no opposition. He who discovers this condition has the privilege of *seeing* the unity of life, of understanding how consciousness has become so vast as to embrace the whole of existence. The entities and the planes are not outside but within oneself, because there is no outside and therefore no inside. Oneness *is*, and it is everywhere in its indivisibility.

Prājña is assimilated to deep dreamless sleep, because in *prājña* everything goes back to silence, to non-becoming, to non-motion.

Therefore, waking, dreaming and deep dreamless sleep correspond to *vaiśvānara*, *taijasa* and *prājña*; and as waking, dreaming and deep sleep are experienced by a single witness, so *vaiśvānara*, the gross state, *taijasa*, the subtle state, and *prājña*, the germinal or causal

---

[1] Plotinus, *Enneads*, I, 8, II, op. cit.

state, are all experienced by one and the same witness (*sākśin*), the only real and constant factor, while the three states appear and disappear. This witness, also called *avaśthātraya sākśin* (witness of the three states) is the reflection, at the level of the manifest, of the transcendent *Brahman* or *ātman* (the Fourth) beyond the three states, while at the same time permeating them.

Q. Have these states a correspondence with other traditional Branches?

A. Yes, according to the Mystery Tradition synthesized by Plotinus, we have three states or dimensions which represent the realm of the formal and non-formal manifestation, as well as a fourth called the metaphysical One, which is beyond the Spirit or Being itself.

In the *Corpus Hermeticum* (X, 14) it is said:

'All things depend upon a single principle, and this principle depends on the One and Only [that is, on the One without a second of the *Vedānta* Tradition]. While the principle is in movement in order to become principle again, the One and Only remains still and is not subject to movement.'

MĀYĀ

Q. What is meant by the term *māyā*?

A. The term has a number of different meanings according to the point of view of the different *vedāntic* currents. Thus, phenomenon, *prakṛti* or nature, *śakti*, *avidyā*, that which renders possible the impossible, taking one thing for another, veiling superimposition, etc., all refer to *māyā*.

Q. What is meant, for example, by 'veiling superimposition'?

A. It means superimposing one datum upon another, thus taking one thing to be something else.[1] For example, we can superimpose the colour blue upon the sky, which is really colourless. We can superimpose the physical body upon the pure *ātman* so that we fall into the error of considering the physical body absolute and real. We can superimpose a concept, formulated by the mind, upon a reality whose nature is actually different. Thus for a long time we held a concept of matter which we have had to rectify. This implies that we superimposed an erroneous idea upon the datum called 'matter'.

---

[1] For superimposition (*adhyāsa*), see the Introduction by Śaṅkara to the *Brahmasūtra* of Bādarāyaṇa. Collezione Vidyā.

Superimposition is caused by two factors: the projecting factor – with our imagination we *project* an idea, a concept, etc. – and the veiling factor, because the projection veils and hides the reality of the datum. In fact, the blue colour that we have projected upon the sky obviously hides the true nature of the sky, just as the concept of the physical body, which we have projected upon the *ātman*, has the effect of hiding the true nature of the *ātman*.

Māyā is not a real, absolute datum and does not belong to the category of tangible objects, but it can be recognized by simple ascertainment. For example, we might easily take a piece of rope – if we saw it lying in a country lane – to be a snake; in this case we have superimposed the concept or image of 'snake' upon the rope, which is not the snake. But on looking more carefully we recognize, or ascertain, that the snake does not exist and what really exists is a rope. Who fooled us? *Māyā*. From this standpoint we can say that the projection of the snake is the outcome of an error of perception, the effect of not knowing, the fruit of *avidyā* (ignorance concerning the true *nature* of a thing).[1]

Q. What is meant by saying that *māyā* is synonymous with *prakṛti* or nature?

A. *Prakṛti* is the equivalent of *natura naturans*, of substance, of 'matter' (in a special sense), of the universal Mother that produces bodies, forms of all sizes and degrees.

---

[1] For a deeper understanding of *māyā*, the reader is referred to the chapters 'Appearance-*māyā*' (*ślokas* 108-113) and 'The mystery of appearance-*māyā*' of *Vivekacūḍāmaṇi*, op. cit.

It is the plastic and eternal substance (as a pole of essence) from which all created things are made. Just as a body or form (such as a cloud in the sky or a mineral or vegetable body) which is born, grows, and dies represents a phenomenon, so *māyā* or *prakṛti* is a producer of phenomena: all we see around us is phenomenon; it is *māyā* or *prakṛti.*

This *prakṛti* or matter – as we now know – not only undergoes endless change, but can resolve itself into other levels of energetic density; mass can resolve itself into energy and physical energy into subtle, super-physical energy, or into non-matter. All bodies and planes of existence are made of the stuff of *māyā* or *prakṛti. Māyā* is therefore synonymous with *prakṛti*, with phenomenon, with movement or change, since a body is the result of a particular *movement* of *māyā.*

Śakti is the name given to nature in movement.

Q. Then we are all *māyā* or *śakti*?

A. If the human individual were made of only the physical body, we would be obliged to give a positive answer. The dense physical body of man is *māyā*, because it is matter, phenomenon. It is born, it grows and dies; it is subject therefore to transformation, change, dissolution. This is the conception of the materialist who considers matter to be absolute reality.

But according to the traditional Philosophy, man is not merely *māyā* or *prakṛti*: he is also *puruṣa*, that is, *ātman*, Spirit, Essence or Being. We therefore have the polarity of *puruṣa* and *prakṛti*; we have Being, which employs substance or quantity to express qualities. When the *puruṣa* withdraws from its manifest body, the body remains inert, devoid of intelligence, of will and of self-consciousness. Intelligence and will, like self-consciousness, are consubstantial aspects of the *puruṣa*, while *prakṛti*, *māyā*, or substance is only 'sentient'. The *puruṣa* can detach itself from its physical body of manifestation and perceive clearly how its material instrument is something other than itself. Moreover, it can be aware, in an intelligent way, of being able to operate, manifest and express itself at other existential levels beyond the dense physical level.

Q. What does the physical body represent, then, for the *puruṣa* or essence?

A. A body, whatever its size or level may be, is an instrument of contact and of expression capable of operating at an existential level of life. To live and operate upon the dense physical plane, for example, we must have a body capable of expression or an instrument capable of establishing relations with that existential plane. However, the body is only an instrument of contact which can be taken up or dropped.[1]

Q. Is man therefore made of the dualism of being and non-being, essence and substance?

A. Earlier we talked of *polarity* which resolves itself into a transcendental and metaphysical point, where polarity or what we conceptually call being and non-being disappear.

---

[1] Cf. *Vivekacūḍāmaṇi*, *ślokas* 154 and 155, op. cit.

Q. If even *māyā* or *prakṛti* is a polarity of the metaphysical Point, why are we told to reject *māyā* or *prakṛti*?

A. The metaphysics of Non-duality does not tell us to desert, reject, or negate *māyā*; such an attitude belongs to the sphere of *avidyā*. What *asparśa* metaphysics tells us is not to create identification or identify with *māyā*, not to superimpose *māyā* upon *puruṣa* or the metaphysical Point, taking – as in the classical example – the rope for the snake.

If we believe ourselves to be exclusively body, vehicle, form (and therefore *prakṛti*), we fall into *avidyā*, that is, we fall into the error of considering as absolute that which is not absolute or to consider that which is *imperishable* and *constant* as changeable and perishable. The disharmony, aberration and chaos of human individuality derive from the fact that the individual considers himself to be only body and form, and therefore a limitation, since each body represents a limitation or bondage of the being.

Q. Can *avidyā* be considered absolute, real, and permanent?

A. If it were real or absolute, we could never eliminate it, and so we would be obliged to remain in incompleteness and ignorance; we would always remain in error, without any hope of escape.

Q. And where does *avidyā* go when it is resolved?

A. It comes from nowhere and it goes nowhere. When we discover that the rope is not a snake, where does the error go? Or when we wake up, where has the world of dreams gone, the world that is projected upon the screen of our 'aura' and made of the stuff of *prakṛti* or substance?

Here is what Śaṅkara says:

> 'Where has the universe gone to? Who has made it vanish? Scarcely had I become aware of it than it vanished. O wonders of mirages!'[1]

When we manifest an idea, a thought, we form a definite and geometrical mental image that a discerning clairvoyant can see.

Now, when shall we stop wondering where the form or image goes? This entire phenomenal universe is an *idea* materialized by *Mahat* (universal Mind) and, when the supreme *puruṣa* stops 'ideating', the universe vanishes like a cloud in the sky.

We have to eliminate two types of identification or superimposition which are the products of *avidyā*, but which are also two moments of the same process: one is when we believe ourselves to be image, form, or body; the other when we believe ourselves to be *prakṛti* at the non-formal or undifferentiated stage; we, as *puruṣa*, and more so as metaphysical Point, are beyond the world of names and forms, beyond *prakṛti* or substance itself.

Prakṛti is the instrumental cause of the world of names and forms; it is the stuff which the individual and the universal 'dreams' are made of; *puruṣa*, by contrast, is the first cause of the movement of *prakṛti*.

The profound and consciential recognition of what we really are is the goal of Śaṅkara's *Advaita* and Gauḍapāda's *Asparśavāda*.

---

[1] *Ibid*., *śloka* 483.

Conflict, disharmony and pain come to an end only with the recognition of one's own identity. A society of individuals who do not acknowledge their most profound and elementary reality is destined to live in alienation and conflict, notwithstanding all the philosophical, socio-political and sentimental formulae it can create in time and space; time and space represent another name for *māyā*.

Q. Can *māyā*, therefore, solve the eternal problem of being and non-being, of ego and non-ego, and provide an answer to the question of how the Absolute has fallen into the relative?

A. Yes. Every duality (real and non-real, being and non-being, ego and non-ego, absolute and relative, etc.) is the outcome of mental representation: it is neither real nor absolute, neither *ipseity* nor *aseity.*

Between Being and what we believe to be non-being there is *māyā*; it is sufficient to eliminate it to discover that only the absolute Being exists.

Between the rope and the snake or between the dreaming entity and the dream, there is *māyā*; it is sufficient to eliminate it to discover that only the rope or the dreaming entity exists.

The Absolute, if it is such, cannot fall into the relative or transform itself into the relative, just as the absolute Good, if it is such, cannot become evil or anything else; what changes is not Reality in itself, but our perspective of Reality or *māyā*. The rope remains a rope, but what changes (movement) is our perspective, our vision of the snake, of the trickle of water, of a stick, etc., which we superimpose upon the rope.

Q. Can *māyā* be considered pure illusion?

A. *Māyā* is not an illusion in the Western sense of the word. An illusion produces nothing; it is non-existent. An illusory event can be compared to a hare's horns. Śaṅkara holds that the universe of *māyā* is not like the hare's horns or the barren woman's child. In Western terms we can say that *māyā* is synonymous with phenomenon, with 'configuring and configured movement'.

EXPERIENCER AND EXPERIENCED

Q. What are the experiencer and the experienced? Is there something besides this duality? What can they mean from a metaphysical point of view?

A. By looking at man's behaviour one can infer that his movements and decisions are characterized by the *experience* factor. It is commonly accepted that the individual is here on this plane of life to have experiences and feel 'sensations'. Even some spiritualist currents propose 'experience' as the aim and purpose of spirituality, holding that experience produces knowledge and realization.

We should therefore conclude, on the basis of these concepts, that the human being determines himself, develops, knows, etc., through experience.

Experience as such is the result of a movement of qualities (*guṇas*) requiring expression. Feeling, desire, instinct, self-assertion, creative energy, etc., are human qualities that lead to experience. These qualities, when expressed and manifested, improve the individual's *faculties* and develop his specific abilities, thereby broadening his sphere of action.

But who is it that experiences? Who *needs* to experience?

Experience requires an object to be experienced, a quality that tends to express itself, to create activity, or to experience, and a subject that is the enjoyer of the experience. Who, then, is the experiencer?

In psychological terms we may answer that this is the ego. The ego seeks experience through qualities to be expressed, so as to feel gratified and complete.

When we fulfil any desire that is expressed through a quality, the ego enjoys it, but it may not feel satisfied and may even feel frustrated if the *object* of its desire is no longer present. This means that experience is not always pleasant or gratifying.

Someone may well advance the hypothesis that such a dual condition of frustration and gratification (in other words, pleasure and pain) might represent the ego's growth factor. At this point we should try to gain a clear understanding of what this ego is which is in search of experience, of gratification and frustration, or is experiencing duality.

All traditional Branches consider being, in its totality, as made of three aspects: Spirit, soul and body. In *Vedānta* terms these three are called *ātman*, *jīva* and *sthūla*. Which is, then, the aspect of being that seeks experiences or gratification and frustration?

The *ātman* or pure Spirit, being the Absolute in us, cannot seek experience because it is not subject to the laws of *necessity*. That which is complete in itself cannot be in need of anything. The sun cannot need or desire light, for it is itself light; in the same way, the knower cannot desire knowledge if he himself is knowledge.

Therefore the experiencer cannot be the pure Spirit, the *ātman*. This means that in order to find the experiencer we have to go down to other existential levels, where the Soul or the *jīvātman* manifests itself.

The Soul – the Spirit's reflection of consciousness, or a ray of the *ātman*'s fire – expresses itself on three existential levels: that called gross, that called subtle or universal, and that which is principial and noetic. These are the three levels of manifestation mentioned by all branches of the Tradition.

The Soul, on the upper subtle and principial plane, does not experience sensorially but is 'contemplation', while the *ahaṁkāra*, or the sense of ego, having fallen to the lower subtle and gross planes (lower *taijasa* and *viśva*), acts, is spurred to produce, to create activity, to move outside of itself so as to be able to experience.

We should now make a distinction between the 'actionless action', of which the *Gīta* speaks, and simple doing or the promotion of interested and finalized activism.[1] According to the Western Mystery Tradition, we should distinguish between *theoria* and *poiêsis*.

Pure *theoria* does not produce movement, and it does not even produce experience. It is not *necessity*. Pure *theoria*, which is contemplation – to be taken in its true meaning – is only a response of the being to life.

Contemplation – with the meaning given to it by traditional Philosophy – is characterized by the *sattva* quality, or harmony; it is not desire, quest, acquisition, and it is not motivated by physical or psychological interest. Contemplation is pure will, actuation; in actuation Being reveals itself without any dual psychological motivation; Being *is*, act *is*.

Sensorial action is, on the other hand, peculiar to the *ahaṁkāra*, to the empirical ego, which, living under the law of necessity and 'corruption', *must* do, *must* act, *must* move, projecting itself endlessly into the object.

---

[1] See *Bhagavadgītā*, op. cit.

Sensorial action is permeated by *rajas*. Activity carried to its extreme becomes *activism*, action for action's sake, action because one cannot stay still. Action leads to agitation. It is translational movement in the direction of the object to be acquired, while contemplation is a rotating movement around one's own axis.

In pure action, or actuation, we have, paradoxically, non-action or non-doing, as it is a simple unveiling of Being, while in emotional activity we have self-forgetfulness and self-loss in what is experienced or in the object of experience. In empirical activity there is effort, oblivion of one's own true and deepest nature, there is becoming, and there is time and space. Doing or agitation belongs to the empirical ego; pure action is an *act* of the Soul. Doing implies loss of the 'noumenality' of being; actionless action is pure noetic act.

All empirical experiences are non-realities; they are *saṁsāra*. Only That which is behind the experience and the experiencer is the ultimate Reality.

Pure action for the East is *līlā*; for the West, as we have seen, it is *theoria*.

'Contemplation, in its universal meaning, is the act by which each being takes up its place within the hierarchy of the cosmos, attaining its own nature from the illuminating presence of the beings that precede it and propagating its reflections around itself to develop the beings that are below it. Contemplation, in fact, is an 'act unto itself', beyond any exterior or passionate impulse.' (P. Prini, *Plotino*. Vita e Pensiero, Milan).

'And hence the need for both [subject and object of knowledge] to be truly one. But this denotes a *living*

> *contemplation*, that is, contemplation whose object is something that does not exist *in something other.* In fact, when the object is in another, then the other is what lives, for the object is not *alive in itself*.'[1]

According to Plotinus, contemplation is being and actuation all at once: it is *theoria* and *poiêsis* transposed to intelligible planes.

It is necessary, however, to point out that experience, motivated by psychological doing, cannot lead to Being but goes on endlessly on the plane of becoming. It can improve individuated faculties, it can sharpen astuteness, it can lead to *manasic* or mental development, it can give power, but it cannot grant freedom, fulfilment, enlightenment, or contemplation.

> 'Two birds, inseparable friends and with similar names, dwell together on the same tree. One feeds on the fruits of the *pippala*, while the other, without eating, embraces everything with its gaze.'[2]

> 'The soul, which comes from the divine, stays quietly in its abode, abiding steadfastly within itself; but the body, on account of its weakness, becomes agitated and loses itself, either through its own nature or because it is battered by external blows; and it cries out to the common maker of living things and imparts its disturbance to the whole.'[3]

---

[1] Plotinus, *Enneads*, III, 8, VIII, op. cit.

[2] *Muṇḍaka Upaniṣad*, III, 1, 1. Cf. also *Śvetāśvatara Upaniṣad*, IV, 6-7.

[1] Plotinus, *Enneads* VI, 4, XV, op. cit.

The first bird is the *jīva* or individuated spirit, characterized by action, by doing, by acquiring, and by experiencing the fruits of pleasure and pain; the other is the motionless *ātman*, characterized by *summa pax*, by being what it is.

THE 'FALL' OF THE SOUL

Q. Empirical science holds that man comes from below, developing through a series of transformations and evolutionary processes spread out over time.

Sacred Science, on the other hand, holds that man comes from above and that if he is now in this world of conflict this is due to the so-called 'fall'. How can we solve this problem?

A. The problem is certainly challenging and by no means easy to solve if one wishes to examine it using only simple sensory instruments. Is man, then, the outcome of evolution or of involution? Is he the product of becoming or Being?

Again, if man is composed of spirit or *noûs*, soul or *psyché*, and body or *sôma*, to which of these elements must we attribute the evolutionary process?

Scientific empiricism defines man as an assemblage of organs which produce intelligence, will, perception, and consciousness. In other words, according to this scientific philosophy, man, being a body, a form, a complex, cannot but undergo mutation and development. Thus, the human physical structure of the Paleolithic era is not identical to that of the present day.

Sacred Science has no argument against this point. Every form is change, process, and becoming. But the being is not merely *sôma*, body, cell: it is also *noûs*, it is also *psyché*, to use terms belonging to the Western Tradition; it is also Soul, which pre-exists the body and therefore survives after the dissolution of the body.

Parapsychology and even a number of psychological currents are interested in factors that go beyond the physical level.

The problem may be seen from a different angle: does the *noûs*, the Spirit, the *ātman*, or in other words, Being evolve?

Put in this way, the enquiry of evolution or involution posits the issue of Being and becoming or non-being.

What is it that becomes, and what is it that does not?

Elsewhere we examined at some length the problem of Being and non-being and we also considered the impossibility for Being or pure Spirit to evolve.

Here we may consider the concept of fall. In fact, Tradition speaks of the Soul's 'fall', which implies that the Soul comes from Above.

But what is meant by 'fall'? And who has fallen?

It is held by some that man is a 'stunned God', by others that he is a 'fallen Angel', which is really the same thing; others hold that man, having disobeyed his Creator, has been banished to a world of conflict;[1] and yet others that, as he had freedom of choice, he has imprisoned himself with his own hands. There are other points of view, but we can draw some conclusions.

From a philosophical rather than a mystical point of view, the 'fall' may be taken to mean the scission of something that was once whole and integral. This scission may produce oblivion of one's original oneness, thus gen-

---

[1] Cf. the chapter 'Original Sin and Christianity' in *Beyond Doubt*, by Raphael. Aurea Vidyā, New York.

erating duality. Unity is divided and the being, no longer a synthesis, is compelled to wander (movement) until it rediscovers its unity. The one has fallen into the two, and therefore into multiplicity, and in multiplicity there can be no synthesis and no homogeneity, that is, no completeness. The scission is an act of alienation.

If a human being, at a purely psychological level, were to be divided, his case would become pathological because, by losing his original individual identity, he would be forced to live in uncertainty and bewilderment. We can say that such a person would live like a ghost, a sleeper, or a sleep-walker. In this way the individual, by dividing himself, has identified with his phenomenal ghost, with his instruments of contact, with his vehicles or bodies of manifestation, forgetting what we may call his divine counterpart. Some say that man has two selves, his divine Self and his individual self.

Restless, constantly on the move, violent and troubled, man goes in search of his forgotten *half*, in search of his own oneness and completeness. His restlessness is lawful: what is not lawful is the direction that it takes.

The human being, although for ever seeking for his other half outside himself in the world of objects, will never be happy. Although he gives in to his restlessness by acquiring material wealth, by self-assertion, by thirsting for power, and engaging in wars, sex, family, etc., he will never be happy. He may forget himself, he may lose himself indefinitely in objects of all kinds, but he will never be happy and at peace, because he is without his other half. This is a fact and a piece of evidence that needs no demonstration. Until he becomes *re-integrated*, he may become master of the whole world, but he cannot be at peace and serene: he will always feel incomplete, unfulfilled, dissatisfied and will undoubtedly be missing something else. This impelling urge to *search* is so strong because oneness – never truly extinguished in the individual – demands oneness. Every human desire is indicative of something missing, and although man may give in to it he will never feel satisfied unless and until such a desire is turned into an aspiration for unity.

Desire is restlessness, psychological movement; it is a burning need for satisfaction in order to gratify the maimed 'half' that thirsts for completeness. Desire comes from scission and can be resolved only by putting the two halves together again.

From what has been said we can deduce that the demagogues to be feared most are those who try to offer up the things of this phenomenal, material world to this part of being, to this half of the individual, which is eagerly looking for its happiness or its completeness, making him believe that they represent the solution to his problem. It is the vision of the golden calf. In modern times this scission has widened and, as a consequence, the thirst for things (which are not) has grown.

Q. If the pure *ātman* or spirit can never fall into duality, who has been divided then?

A. All the traditional Branches agree in maintaining that the scission concerns the Soul, or *jīvātman* or *psyché* which is a reflection of the pure Spirit. Just as the individual of dream, who experiences duality, is a projection of the mind, so too the Soul is a mere projection of the *ātman*.

Q. How does the scission occur?

A. This projection or reflection of the *ātman* attracts matter to itself from the various planes of existence and makes vehicles or bodies of manifestation from it; then it *identifies* with these bodies, forgetting its true origin. The myth of Narcissus explains this phenomenon and this process very well.[1] We can understand all this only through images and analogies.

Q. Is the individual, a shadow of *ātman*, obliged to identify with its other 'shadow'?

A. He is not obliged, but he is free to do so.

Q. Can you give an example by way of illustration?

A. In our mind we can conjure up an ideal, a passion, etc., and identify with it to such an extent as to forget we are individuals above and beyond passions and ideas. We can dream while wide awake (and wakefulness is also a dream) and we can identify with our dreams to such a degree that we lose our identity. This happens to the majority of people; in fact, they are not Persons, but merely teachers, politicians, tradesmen, fathers, mothers, children, etc.; they are everything and anything but entities aware of their true and profound reality.

When we become one with what we are not or with 'things' – and even our bodies, an ideal, an emotion are things – the scission has taken place. When we have become a 'thing' ourselves, then we have lost both our identity and our freedom.

We may even say that by identifying with an object we have 'fallen', that we are no longer ourselves apart

[1] Cf. Plotinus, *Enneads*, I, 6, VIII; IV, 3, XII.

from being number and quality. 'Oblivion is therefore his wickedness' (*Corpus Hermeticum*: X, 15).

Q. Can the individual then avoid creating the scission?

A. We have said that he may or may not do so: it depends on his *freedom* to be, which is inherent in his nature.

However, we should remember that Being is by nature an indivisible unity that cannot split or *become* two. Thus it is obvious that the scission (a word which undoubtedly is inadequate to express the concept we wish to propose) is not in an absolute sense a loss of balance in the unity, but the nature of Being is such that it can manifest an unlimited number of expressions: the fall or the scission must not be considered as becoming other than Being, but as representing a *mode* of being. A piece of ice is an expression and a mode of water, but one cannot say that an absolute scission or an irreversible fall has occurred in water. Human experience is a mode of being, a state of consciousness of Being.

Q. The fall is not an act of divine will, then?

A. No. Man is divided because he wants to be. He is passionate because he so desires. He is born upon this plane of existence because he so desires. Man is even an individual because he so desires.

Q. So is the Tradition simply pointing to the solution of this scission?

A. Yes. The Tradition is the depositary of this fundamental truth. It teaches the restless, conflicting individual how to find the way back to unity. Traditional symbolism refers to this process of scission and its consequent reintegration; this is the symbolism of Isis and Osiris in ancient Egypt and of Orphism in Greece.[1] In other words, it is the symbolism of the Sacred Mysteries of the West as well as that of the *Vedas* and *Upaniṣads*.

The initiatory death and rebirth are nothing more than a profound symbol. It is necessary to die to what one is not in order to be reborn to what one really is. While the philosophy of becoming perpetuates the state of scission and conflict, the Philosophy of being resolves it by bringing the being back to Being.[2]

> 'What is it, then, which has made the souls forget their father, God, and be ignorant of themselves and him, even though they are parts which come from his higher world and altogether belong to it? The beginning of evil for them was audacity and coming to birth and the first otherness and the wishing to belong to themselves. Since they were clearly delighted with their own independence, and made great use of self-movement, running the opposite course and getting as far away as possible, they were ignorant even that they themselves came from that world; just as children who are immediately torn from their parents and brought up far away do not know who they themselves or their parents are. Since they do not any more see their father or themselves, they despise themselves through ignorance of their birth and honour other things, admiring everything rather than themselves and, astonished and delighted

---

[1] Cf. the chapter 'Orphic Ascesis' in *Orphism and the Inititory Tradition*, by Raphael, op. cit.

[2] Cf. 'The Philosophy of Being' in *Beyond Doubt*, by Raphael, op. cit.

by and dependent on these [earthly] things, they broke themselves loose as far as they could in contempt of that from which they turned away; so that their honour for these things here and their contempt for themselves is the cause of their utter ignorance of God. For what pursues and admires something else admits at the same time its own inferiority; but making itself inferior to things which come into being and perish and considering itself the most contemptible and the most liable to death of all the things which it admires it could not possibly have any idea of the nature and power of God.'[1]

'Here lies the essence of all truly human evil, which consists in *breaking away from the basis of one's being*, in the r*efusal of one's true origin* and in *atheistic alienation.* Plotinus' teaching is, essentially, a therapy for returning to oneself, an exhortation to engage in interior reflection so as to open up selfish closeness (*the will to belong to oneself*) and put a stop to the waste caused by unruly passions (*running the opposite course*).

'Selfishness is no more than a failing of the original power of love and liberality which is the essence of every spiritual being. It is a fault 'due to lack of vigour', a degradation and corruption of the deepest human energy no longer able to elevate itself, within the most intimate recess of the mind where the sense of the Sacred abides. Thus passions, instead of being mere 'alterations' of the body, become 'agitations' of the soul, deviating it, as in a dream, from its true life; they all arise from a debasement of Eros, from its becoming 'earthly' and forgoing

---

[1] Plotinus, *Enneads*, V, 1, 1, op. cit.

that true love of man for his own *dignitas* and for the beauty of his own soul.

'The way of liberation, according to Plotinus, lies in the purification of our inner sight (I, 6, VIII) so that the soul may recognize itself in all its original decorum.' (Pietro Prini, *Plotino*, Vita e Pensiero, Milan, op. cit.)

WHAT IT IS THAT TRANSMIGRATES

Q. People speak of reincarnation, of metempsychosis, rebirth, transmigration. What do these terms mean? And who is it that is reborn or transmigrates?

A. All the Branches of Tradition have faced the problem of rebirth. The Western Mystery Tradition speaks of metempsychosis, the Oriental – in which Buddhism, Taoism and Jainism may be included – of transmigration or rebirth.

The concept of transmigration or rebirth obviously implies that there is something which leaves and which comes back, something which creates movement or changes condition. Further questions may be asked: why does one transmigrate, why is one reborn? This point is very important and very much discussed.

First of all, let us restate the problem in metaphysical terms: that which is 'born', if it really is so, cannot be born a second time; that which is not born cannot be born or come into existence, because it is an eternal presence, an absolute or a constant. The non-existent cannot be born or exist or be.

Therefore, if the Constant or *ātman*, the pure Spirit, the Absolute in us or the pure Being cannot be born because it simply *is*, nor transmigrate because it is not subject to change, then what is it in us that transmigrates? And why does it transmigrate; why is it reborn?

In order to understand who is reborn and why, we must know the makeup of the manifested entity in its psycho-physical components; in this way we shall be able to examine the whole problem in all its aspects.

As we have already seen, according to the Western Mystery Tradition man is a synthesis of *noûs*, *psyché* and *sôma*; according to the *Vedānta* Tradition he is a synthesis of *ātma*, *jīva* and *jīvabhūta*. The *noûs*, like the *ātma*, being the constant, the immortal, the non-born and the absolute in us, cannot, of course, be subject to birth and transmigration. The immortal cannot become mortal, nor can the mortal become immortal, as Gauḍapāda states in his *kārikās* to the *Māṇḍūkya Upaniṣad*.

The body or bodies of the entity, being as perishable as flies, disintegrate, and their elements return to the existential plane from which they have been drawn. They cannot transmigrate or be reborn because, being compounds, they dissolve and disintegrate, leaving no trace behind them.

The *jīva* or *psyché* is a reflection of consciousness of the *ātma* or *noûs*. It is a ray of pure consciousness which, though being a mere ray, has within itself being and will, consciousness and intelligence, and creativity. It attracts to itself a certain amount of substance from the existential planes of Being, producing its *bodies* of manifestation through which it can experience the various objects of the senses.

> 'An eternal fragment of Me, having appeared as a living soul (*jīvabhūta*) in the world of the mortals, attracts towards itself the [five] senses and the mind

(*manas*) as the sixth organ, all of which find their foundation in *prakṛti*.'[1]

If the *ātma* belongs to the state of Being and therefore, being immortal, cannot transmigrate, if the body belongs to the condition of non-being, and therefore has no life of its own or *aseity*, then we must turn our attention to two very important factors: the reflection, *jīva*, *psyché* and the qualities which represent the 'fragrance' of the substance.

'The vital breath', writes René Guénon, paraphrasing a number of chapters of the *Bṛhadāraṇyaka Upaniṣad*, *Chāndogya Upaniṣad* and *Brahmasūtra*, which deal with the question of death, 'accompanied by all its other functions and faculties (already re-absorbed into it and not subsisting in it except as possibilities, having now reverted to the state of non-differentiation from which they had to emerge in order to actually manifest themselves during life) is in turn re-absorbed into the living soul (*jīvātman*, the particular manifestation of the Self at the core of human individuality, as already explained, and distinct from the Self so long as that individuality endures as such, though this distinction is an illusion from the standpoint of the absolute reality, for which there is nothing but the Self); and it is precisely this living soul (as the reflection of the Self and central principle of individuality) which governs the whole of the individual faculties (considered in their integrality and not only in their relationship with the corporeal mode). As the servants of a King gather around him when he is about to undertake a journey, even so all the vital functions and faculties of the individual (external and

[1] *Bhagavadgītā*, XV, 7, op. cit.

internal) gather around the living soul (or rather within it, from which they all issue and into which they are all re-absorbed) at the last moment (of life, in the ordinary sense of the word, that is, of existence manifested at the gross level), when this living soul is about to leave its corporeal form. Thus, accompanied by all its faculties (as it contains and keeps them as possibilities), it withdraws into a luminous individual essence (that is, into the subtle form, compared to a fiery vehicle, as we have explained with regard to *taijasa*, the second condition of *ātmā*), which is composed of the five *tanmātras* or supra-sensible elementary essences (just as the physical body is compounded of the five *bhūtas* or corporeal and sensible elements), into a subtle state (as opposed to the gross state, which is the state of external or bodily manifestation whose cycle, as far as the individual is concerned, is completed).

'As a result (due to this passage into the subtle form, described as luminous) the vital breath is said to withdraw into the Light, without meaning by this the fiery principle in the exclusive sense (for in reality it concerns an individualized reflection of the intelligible Light, a reflection whose nature is basically the same as that of mental reflection during bodily life and which, on the other hand, implies a combination of the five basic principles of the five elements as its support or vehicle). This withdrawal does not necessarily imply an immediate transition: in fact, (to give an example) a traveller is said to travel from one city to another, even though he may stop at one or more cities in between.

'This withdrawal or departure from the bodily form (as described so far) is common to the ignorant person (*avidvān*) and to the contemplative Sage (*vidvān*), up to the point at which their respective (and from now on different) ways part.'[1]

Q. What are the qualities we spoke about?

A. The qualities – *sattva*, *rajas*, *tamas* – are allotropic states of *prakṛti* (substance or matter). An instinct, a desire, a passion, etc., are prakṛtic qualities; these qualities manifest themselves by means of a body or vehicle and, if coagulated, survive the body. The fragrance lives on in the air even when, for example, a flower has disappeared or the bottle of perfume has broken. A pain or pleasure caused by an event remains even when the event has vanished.

While the *sôma* or *sthūlaśarīra* or *jīvabhūta* supplies the instrument of pleasure and pain or of the qualities, these qualities, when they survive, cling to that reflection of consciousness represented by the experiencer. Let us say that ideals, feelings, instincts, etc., can survive physical death. And as these qualities belong to the psychic dimension we can conclude that the psychic vehicle (which is not the Self) can survive the physical one.

Q. How might we express ourselves in psychological terms?

A. A crystallized psychical content can survive the dissolution of the physical compound. The *Vedānta*

---

[1] R. Guénon, *Man and his becoming according to Vedānta*, by Richard C. Nicholson. Oriental Books Reprint Corporation. New Delhi 1981. For the paraphrased books by Guénon, see *Bṛhadāraṇyaka Upaniṣad*, IV, III, 38, and *Brahmasūtra*, IV, II, 1-7, by Raphael. Aurea Vidyā, New York.

speaks, in fact, of *vāsanās*, of *saṁskāras*, which represent the 'colours', the 'odours', the tendencies, the psychical qualitative predispositions. These tendencies, stored up in our own spatiality and not dissolved, survive the death of the body.[1]

Q. How are the *vāsanās* formed?

A. When the reflection of consciousness experiences and *adheres* to a quality, it produces a *vāsanā*, or a content: the energy coagulates and becomes mass. It is obvious that in this condition the experiencer is determined by the content which, being continually nourished, grows powerful and capable of dominating the experiencer himself. The energetic power of the dream dominates the dreamer.[2]

Q. Then why do we transmigrate?

A. We transmigrate because the unresolved qualitative mass or contents demand expression on the existential plane best suited to allow their maturation and allievation.

Q. But is it the same individual who transmigrates?

A. That individual with a name and a form cannot transmigrate because he no longer subsists on the death of his vehicles. The empirical self is the outcome of the combination of *ahaṁkāra* and vehicle; when the vehicle

[1] For a deeper understanding, see the chapter 'Post Mortem and Bardo Thötröl' in *Beyond Doubt*, by Raphael, op. cit.

[2] Cf. the chapter 'The origin of subconsciousness' in *Tat tvam asi*, by Raphael, op. cit.

disappears, the *ahaṁkāra* returns to its state of potentiality. And when both disappear there is no longer individuality: there is the *person* in his supra-individual state.

The qualities in themselves have no name, nor has the reflection of consciousness a name. The qualities become individualized through the vehicles and the sense of ego (*ahaṁkāra*). A name is the indication of an energetic complex which has assumed individuality, determined itself, and drawn a circle around itself. We can say that in most cases individuals are simply passive *mediums* in the hands of entities or qualities (*guṇas*) in search of expression or maturation.

Q. Is embodiment a school needed for advancing and evolving towards the *ātman*?

A. The one Tradition has never taught the evolutionary concept.

Let us examine the problem in metaphysical terms: because the *ātman* or Being *is* and does not become, it cannot evolve. Qualities do not evolve but simply change aspect: cold and heat do not evolve, just as hate and love do not. Individuality, with a name and form, does not evolve (it may encounter some possible modification) because it is the synthesis of an energetic compound which expresses itself through various qualitative aspects (*guṇas*); it is born and it dies.

Q. Is it proper to speak of reincarnation?

A. It depends on the meaning one wishes to give to the word. Let us say that the question may be posed in different terms. If we consider that the universe or manifestation is composed of three vibratory states or levels which, however, represent a whole, then we may note that the *jīvātman* is now on one existential level and now on another. It passes through changes of state or condition, and these movements – we may call them transmigrations – are caused by the *guṇas* and by the individualized and crystallized *vāsanās*.

Again, we may say that just as an individual, prompted by certain needs and qualities, migrates, for example, from Europe to America, and thus changes his lifestyle, so the reflection of consciousness, prompted by certain qualities, transmigrates from one state to another or from one world (*loka*) to another. There is nothing dramatic or tragic in all this; it is an event that occurs automatically (in the case of the majority of beings), innocently and naturally. If the event is held to be dramatic, often tragic, it is because the entity is not aware of the process of transmigration, or else is a prisoner of a simple fear of change.

Q. So is it not the 'I' of this present time and space that transmigrates?

A. The empirical self is a mere *phenomenon* connected to time and space. The empirical self of one particular moment is not the self of another.

In a particular time and space we can say: *I am happy.* In another time and space, which may be immediately subsequent, we may say: *I am in conflict.* The two egos are not the same, because they annul one another in their contradiction. The empirical self is a contingent factor, an expressive moment of certain qualities (*guṇas*).

Q. Then is it the Soul that reincarnates or transmigrates?

A. According to the Tradition, the Soul itself is a mere reflection of the pure Spirit or *ātman*, and it is a non-absolute; it dwells in a dimension (higher *taijasa*) which is not the dense physical dimension (*viśva*); from that dimension, as we mentioned before, it manifests itself on the lower *taijasa* plane (the *astral* plane of Western occultism) and on the *viśva* (dense physical) plane through one of its rays of Consciousness. Its movement (transmigration) produces expressions of qualities, causes and effects. If the empirical I – related to the dense physical body, to the vital body (*prāṇa*) and to the mental body – is a mere contingent factor, the *jīvātman* is relatively long-lived, so as to appear eternal to the empirical ego. But the transmigration or movement of a quality occurs also within the same incarnation.

Q. How can this be possible?

A. For example, a desire is *born* (the beginning of the movement), it tends towards a particular object (path of motion), and it *dies* when it finds satisfaction and maturation. If we assume that the seed or germ (*vāsanā* or *saṁskāra*) of desire is not resolved, gradually a new desire is *born* and transmigrates towards a new object *to die* in it. As long as the root or germ of desire exists, the quality (*guṇas*) transmigrates from one object to another, from one space to another. And obviously the ego-desire of one moment is not that of another, because the empirical I, being becoming or movement, is not constant; in other words, it is not Being, just as the *jīvātman* itself is not Being.

Q. Must these entities or qualities necessarily transmigrate onto the dense physical plane?

A. These crystallized entities or qualities transmigrate wherever they can express and manifest themselves, following the law of attraction and repulsion or of harmonization. In the multiple states of Being there is room for the expression of all the possible *prakṛtic* qualities.

Q. Is there reincarnation for the Liberated?

A. If one is Liberated one can no longer transmigrate. For the Liberated all becoming or movement has ceased; he has returned to his true Homeland ('My Kingdom is not of this world'), and he does not wish to go anywhere; having no *vāsanās* or individualized qualities to express, he has no desire, no past and no future. Transmigration implies that something has been left unfinished, incomplete, but for the one who stands *still*, like the hub of a wheel, there is no more coming and going, no more birth and death, because such events belong to a consciousness that has not yet grasped its own essence.

ANALOGY AND IDENTITY
SYMBOL AND THING SYMBOLIZED

Q. What can an analogy or a symbol represent?

A. In some passages of the *Upaniṣads* we read:

'He (the *ātman*) created these worlds: *ambhas*, *mārīci*, *mara*, and *āpas*. What is beyond the heavens is *ambhas*. The heavens are the foundation. The intermediate space is *mārīci*. The earth is *mara*. What is below are the *āpas*, the shining Rays, Death, the Waters.

'Indeed, the moon is the door to the celestial world (*svarga loka*).

'*Om*. The head of the sacrificial horse is, in truth, dawn; its eye is the sun; its breath is the wind; its open jaws are the *vaiśvānara* fire. The body of the sacrificial horse is the year.'[1]

Elsewhere we read that the universe is composed of earth, air, and sky; or of three states called *Virāṭ*, *Hiraṇyagarbha*, and *Īśvara*, and there is a Fourth state called *Turīya*.

---

[1] *Aitareya Upaniṣad*, I, I, 2; *Kauṣitakı Upaniṣad*, I, 2; *Bṛhadāraṇyaka Upaniṣad*, I, I, 1. See *Upaniṣad*, as presented by Raphael, op. cit.

If we were to take terms such as ocean, space, sky, air or atmosphere, waters, etc., literally, we would arrive at the conclusion that these writings were fables and not very felicitous at that, or that they were Sibylline games for people with nothing to do, or again the myths of a primitive people devoid of common sense. And, indeed, for some people this is what they actually are.

But the fact is that these texts speak of a knowledge of Being and non-being, of the Infinite and of the relative, of noumenon and phenomenon, topics which do not at all belong to primitive minds but to true philosophers (here we shall not speak of the non-human inspiration of certain texts and doctrines).

In the *Bṛhadāraṇyaka Upaniṣad* (the first reading) and in the *Chāndogya Upaniṣad* (VI, II, I), for example, it is stated that Being is the irradiation of Non-Being and that from Being the determinations of phenomenal manifestation emerged. However much one would like us to believe these to be nothing but myths created by primitive minds, we feel we cannot, in all honesty, support such a belief.

> 'From non-being lead me to Being, from darkness lead me to light, from death lead me to immortality'[1]

When we first approach a branch of knowledge – whether or not it be philosophy – in order to interpret it properly we should refer to a number of basic principles, otherwise we risk falling into serious errors of judgement.

First of all, every science has its own peculiar terminology, its own conceptual framework and reference structure, which has to be kept in mind. Furthermore,

---

[1] *Bṛhadāraṇyaka Upaniṣad,* I, III, 2.

the time in which the science or philosophy was drawn up has to be taken into due account. Thus, the Egyptian hieroglyphs are not pictures or simple drawings, but a particular language of the times which corresponds to equally precise ideas, even of a metaphysical order.

We can say that in every age and in every place the different branches of science have had, and continue to have, their own language and their own particular 'hieroglyph'. What else is the chemical formula for water H_2O, but a kind of hieroglyph? And yet this formula contains a basic truth, encloses an idea which only the 'experts' can decipher.

What else are words such as 'air', 'sky', 'golden egg', 'waters', etc., and what are they intended to represent?

When – at the human level – we wish to show or communicate a truth that has been experienced or revealed, the only means we have at our disposal is language, which can take on different possibilities of expression: figurative, analogical, symbolic, discursive, metaphysical, etc.

A traditional or initiatory Teaching is in most cases symbolic, sometimes figurative or analogical. Why? For two fundamental reasons: because by means of symbols, or analogies, it seeks to *evoke* within the disciple the truth that is being symbolized, for initiatory truth is not meant for the analytical mind, but for the heart of the disciple. Besides, symbol and analogy reach beyond time and space. When we express ourselves by means of formulae such as: *the Sun is the living universal God*, this makes it understood that the sun as a symbol is not only valid for us and for those living at the time of the Egyptian king Amenhotep (Akhenaton), but that it is a powerful symbol veiling a metaphysical truth. The analogy between the physical sun and the metaphysical Sun is adequate and is in line with Traditional Science.[1]

It is evident, however, that anyone who does not know the key of Traditional Science may fall into serious error and consider the physical sun as being *identical* with God or with the supreme Being. Analogy does not mean identity, and a symbol, taken at its face value, is an empty image and devoid of meaning. The cross, for example, is a symbol which embraces a precise initiatory truth. More than that: the symbol, being by its very nature succinct, contains a number of different truths, depending upon the level or system of co-ordinates to which one may wish to relate it. Hence arises a whole Science of symbols, which cannot be the object of discursive transmission: and there are many reasons why it cannot be so.

To tell someone that the word-symbol 'sky' – or 'waters', 'golden egg', 'ocean', etc. – encloses a precise state of consciousness, a dimension or a state of Being, is of little use. Reality as such is unspeakable and can only be communicated through symbols, analogies, images, hieroglyphs. If a symbol or analogy succeeds in finding its way into someone's consciousness, it may be able to reveal its esoteric significance.

The *Vedas* and the *Upaniṣads*, just to take one Branch of the philosophical Tradition, or *Philosophia Perennis*, are of a symbolic, analogical, figurative order. Many of its terms, such as *Brahman*, *Ātman*, *Īśvara*, *Jīva*, *Śiva*, etc., are profoundly symbolical: they represent precise states of consciousness, functions, dimensions or realms of Being. To consider *Brahman* to be mere

---

[1] See Plato, *Politéia*, VI, 508-9.

physical water or the physical sun or the air, composed of oxygen and hydrogen, means being very far from the correct interpretation of the symbol.

To believe that the mercury of Alchemy – another branch of the Tradition – is the mercury contained in thermometers to measure the temperature is a sign of ignorance and naivety.[1]

The *ātman* is the atomic nucleus which, although giving life and movement to its electronic shells, remains unaltered and equidistant: this is an analogy, an image, but not an identity. Between the *ātman* and the physical atom there is a great gulf fixed.

The term 'symbol' comes from the Greek word *simbolon* (σύμβολον) and indicates the two halves or corresponding parts of an object kept by two different people as a sign of recognition. *Simbolon* also means 'divine sign', 'password', 'distinctive mark', etc. This suggests the idea that when the two halves are joined together again and match, unity, which is synthesis, is attained once more. When the celestial Ocean and the Earth are reunited, they recognize each other as unity – and the Harmony of the spheres resounds in Space-life.

The contrary of *simbolon* is *diabolos* (from διαβάλλω) which means: to throw across, to calumniate, to oppose, to contrast, to distort, to deceive; in other words, to divide. And that which divides or separates is *ahaṁkāra* or the sense of ego, and *manas* or the empirical mind.

---

[1] See 'Realization according to Alchemy' in T*he Threefold Pathway of Fire*, by Raphael, op. cit.

KARMA OR THE LAW OF CAUSE AND EFFECT

Q. People speak of *karma*, sin, law of retaliation, of reparation, etc. What do these words mean?

A. We have to distinguish what is a philosophical vision of Reality from a vision that is sentimental, anthropomorphous or religious and theistic.

The theistic, anthropomorphous outlook brings God or Being down to the human dimension, endowing it with qualities of love and hate or of attraction and repulsion. God is infinite goodness but He is also the punisher of those who go against His will. Down through the ages many religions have drawn inspiration from this dual God, even if they spoke of 'the one God'.

The relationship between man and God, based upon these assumptions, leads to a stressing of the moral aspect because, according to his conduct, man may conform to or violate the will of God. Sin is a psychological attitude which infringes or violates the law of God. Since moral behaviour implies a set of norms to conform to, anthropomorphous theistic religion has a code, considered to be divine, which each believer must obey. Disobedience is followed by sin; whosoever does not obey or conform to the law sins: hence the 'reparation' which is necessary in order to be permitted back into the 'grace' of the offended God. As religious theism attributes to God alone the principle of will, man is left with the sole choice of obeying or disobeying; yet, although he may obey, the verdict of absolution remains exclusively in the hands of God. God is the arbiter of the entire destiny of mankind, introducing Himself into human affairs in time and space. He may grant or withhold his forgiveness, according to His inscrutable designs.

The *nemesis* of the Sacred Mysteries is the equivalent of the Vedic *karma*. The word *karma* means ritual action, but also the law of cause and effect. What is this law?

At the psycho-spiritual level, just as at the physical level, every effect is the materialization of a cause. We might say that the law of *karma* is similar to that of cause and effect in science.

Man has the possibility of moving in different directions, producing effects which may or may not be in harmony with himself and with others. *Nemesis* consists in re-establishing Order and equilibrium where imbalance and disorder have occurred. By upsetting the balance or creating disharmony in the universal Order the *mystes* (μύστης) receives a repercussion: this is the law of *nemesis* that comes in and operates so that the Order is re-established.

If we put a finger into the fire (cause) the effect will be a burn; however, this does not imply that a vindictive or emotional God has chosen to punish us and applied the law of retaliation: our ignorance (*avidyā*) of a law has led us into *error.*

A powerful energy of hatred or love draws to itself energy of the same nature and strength. The effect is proportionate to the cause. There is nothing extraordinary in the fact that a discharge, let us say, of hate attracts hate: this is the law of magnetic sympathy in action.

When Jesus told us to love those who hate us, he did not wish to enunciate a principle of social and sentimental morality. Rather, he wished to point out a universal law. If hate attracts hate, then in order to neutralize a force of a certain nature and intensity it is necessary to use another of equal and opposite strength. The law of the Initiate is: love your enemy.

Ignorance is overcome by knowledge, inertia by determination, pessimism by optimism, and hate by love.

The law of *karma* or *nemesis* has been laid down by the Sacred Science.

In order to understand certain things properly one has to consider that a dense physical form is a complex of energy with qualities and a producer of causes and effects and that the individual, too, is a centre of consciousness around which qualified energies generating causes and effects revolve. Just as studying physics allows us to know how the mechanism of the law of cause and effect works, so studying the Sacred Science allows us to understand the manner in which the law of *karma* operates.

We must recognize the fact that many events, even negative ones, to which we are subjected, are not produced by God but by ourselves, because we are the ones who set the law of *karma* in motion. But if we wish to neutralize a force we obviously need another powerful force to counteract it. This is where many fail, as they believe they do not possess sufficient energy capable of producing a contrary cause.

In order to overcome the earth's gravitational force, man has had to use not only a force equal and opposite to it, but also a 'quantum' of extra energy by which to transcend it altogether. The universe, at all levels, is governed by laws (*dharma*) and a correct understanding of the law can give the individual the possibility not only of *harmonizing* with nature but also – and this is a consequence – of positively making harmonious what we call his own destiny.

The sorrow and conflict in man's world is not brought about by a capricious and emotional God, but by man himself who has not yet understood the operative dynamics of some of the laws governing the universe and the individual.

Man can use, manipulate, and direct forces and energies, but he alone is responsible for the results.

With reference to the individual, *Vedānta* names three kinds of *karma*: *āgāmin*, *saṁcita*, and *prārabdha*. Śaṅkara, in his *Vivekacūḍāmaṇi* (*śloka* 453), says:

> 'The *prārabdhakarma* is too powerful for the realized being to restrain; it will exhaust itself when its fruits come to an end. The other two types of *karma*, that resulting from previous actions (*saṁcita*) and that whose effects have not yet matured (*āgāmin*), will be burnt to ashes by the fire of knowledge. However, none of these three kinds of karma is capable of affecting the ascetic who has realized *Brahman* and lives in identity with It'.[1]

Prārabdhakarma is the matured kind of karma and is therefore the current one: having taken on a physical body is a *prārabdha* because it is a matured *karma*. The physical body is here and we cannot destroy it. To have a child is a *prārabdha* because a child, once it has been brought into being, cannot be sent back.

The other two kinds of *karma*, not having come into objective existence, can be stopped and even extinguished or resolved because the favouring causes have been removed. The cause of the karmic causes is

---

[1] Śaṅkara, *Vivekacūḍāmaṇi*, *śloka* 453, op.cit.

avidyā, the metaphysical ignorance which concerns the nature of Being; when it is resolved, the karma vanishes, and for the *jñāni-asparśin* even the *prārabdha* is as if it did not exist because it has no grasp upon his liberated consciousness.

> 'The *brāhmaṇa*, having recognized that the different worlds are the outcome of accumulated *karma*, feels disgusted with them because one cannot realize the Non-created by means of what is created.'[1]

[1] *Muṇḍaka Upaniṣad*, II, 1, 12.

THE SIDDHIS[1]

Q. When one speaks of *yoga*, or of Eastern teachings, the so-called 'powers' or *siddhis* come immediately to one's mind. But what are these powers?

A. Much confusion and misunderstanding can arise with regard to this particular topic. Apart from the correct attitude of consciousness that is required towards the different kinds of *yoga* or traditional Teachings, we have to recognize the fact that many conceive of Realization as the achievement or acquisition of the so-called 'powers'.

First of all, we must make some distinctions. In psychological terms, a power is a *faculty* or *capacity* inherent in matter itself, and it may be considered as a quality or attribute of it. In philosophical terms 'power' means 'possibility': the possibility of a being to perform or express an act.

We should make a further distinction between what is called a 'psychic power' and a psychological faculty; the latter bears reference more specifically to the mind in general. Mental perception, which everyone has, is a

---

[1] Cf. the chapter '*Vibhūti Pāda*', on the subject of *siddhis*, in *The Regal Way to Realization* by Patañjali, as presented by Raphael. Aurea Vidyā, New York.

psychological faculty which concerns the aspect of *psyché* and not that of *sôma*.

The psychic power as such represents the development of particular senses or sensory organs which grant the ability of 'hearing' and 'seeing' on planes that go beyond the dense physical one. As at the physical level we have the five senses which bring us into contact with the gross, material plane, so too at the subtle, supra-physical level we have other senses which connect us with that existential level or plane.

Besides physical sight we have psychical sight (clairvoyance); besides physical hearing, by means of which we perceive physical sounds, we have psychical hearing (clairaudience) by which we perceive subtle sounds which are beyond the range of physical hearing. We can say that a psychic power is a faculty of the psyche existing as a reality that is independent of the physical body or *sôma*.

The majority seek psychic powers for two reasons:

1) because, being a simple extension of the empirical self upon the subtle psychical plane, the self is not hampered by them: rather it is magnified and strengthened. The majority seek the expansion of their ego, not its solution and transcendence.

2) because they represent a compensation for the weakness, failings and limitations of individuality.[1]

Similarly, at the physical level many go after wealth, which is a material *power*, in order to feel stronger, more confident, and ego-centred. Not having found security and

---

[1] Cf. 'Occultism and psychic powers' in *At the Source of Life*. Aurea Vidyā. New York.

peace of mind within themselves, they compensate for this failing through wealth. In fact, we know that wealth becomes an all-important compensation for those who *are not*. Even intellectual 'power' may be a compensation. The wealth given by the psychic power meets this need; it compensates for many a deficiency and many a lack in the empirical self because, in truth, the ego *is not*.

However, if psychic powers belong to the ego, and the worldly ego (as it is often defined in order to distinguish it from the Self or spirit) is marked by incompleteness, by lack, and by relativity, then the powers inherent in it belong to the realm of *avidyā*, to use *Vedānta* terminology.

An entity may be clairvoyant, clairaudient, able to levitate, telepathic, psychometric, etc., but this is of little importance because such a person belongs to and moves within the sphere of *avidyā*.

Those who are after the psychical power for its own sake may represent interesting subjects for psychoanalysis. At times these persons waste an entire existence in order to become mediocre clairvoyants, sensitives, mediums, etc.

With reference to psychic powers there is a very revealing anecdote concerning the Buddha. As the story goes, one day, as the Buddha entered a wood, he met a meditating 'santon'. On seeing the Buddha, he went out to meet him and asked him to express his opinion about the ascetic practices he had carried on for so many years.

A large river was nearby and the santon, raising himself up into the air, crossed over the waters. When he came back into the presence of the Buddha, he urged him to say something. The Buddha, not in the least ruffled, asked, 'How long has it taken you to acquire the power of levitating?' The santon answered, 'Twenty years'. And the Buddha rejoined, 'With five rupees I can cross this river in a boat in as few as five minutes'.

Power is not Realization of the *ātman* because, being a *faculty*, it belongs to *prakṛti*. All power operates within the sphere of duality. It involves an entity who wields the power, the power itself, and an object to which the power is applied. Power, by operating in the dual and multiple world, cannot be the source of *ānanda* or the source of *Completeness* or *Pax profunda*, which is inherent in Being.

The greatest power that can be attained is that of Illumination, *satori*, *paravidyā*, and gnosis. This power does not belong any longer to the psychic realm but to the strictly spiritual one. In this sphere the individual, with all his toy-powers, no longer exists because he is completely transcended.

Q. However, we know of true Saints who use powers.

A. They are Saints not because they make use of powers but because they are Illuminated. If occasionally they use some psychic faculties, it is to make an emotional impression upon the masses – who in fact need such things – rather than to indicate the pathway of Illumination.

A Saint may make use of a power as a temporary means by which to draw the attention of unbelievers, while mere individuality needs power as psychological compensation and as an end.

Q. You said before that a power is a faculty which influences the environment. What difference is there between this influence and that of the Saint?

A. The difference is great indeed. The influence of a power acts:

1) on the psycho-physical (individualized) plane;
2) on the plane of force, energy;
3) within the field of subject and object duality;
4) on the plane of the ego's will;
5) in order to obtain a physical or psychological advantage.

The influence of the Realized one operates:

1) on the spiritual (universal) plane;
2) on the plane of 'innocence', of non-resistance. The influence of the Realized one is an emanation that expands naturally, like the fragrance of a flower;
3) within the field of pure Subject, because it does not pay any attention to the object. The Realized one does not try or seek or desire to influence others;
4) on the plane of non-will, non-desire, because it has no selfish aims;
5) and therefore on the plane of 'gift', of pure Love, since it is his own particular conscious vibration that resounds.

Thus, while psychic powers operate in the sphere of individualized existence, spiritual power acts within the sphere of the supra-individual or the universal.

The influence of the Realized one becomes a 'magnetic field' at the centre of the *world*, while that of the psyche is merely a relationship between a single subject and an object.

Q. Can we say, therefore, that the Realized one 'vibrates' *sat-cit-ānanda*, while the person who has psychic powers must use a force, a faculty, in order to obtain certain effects?

A. Yes, indeed. The Realized one is pure Consciousness without superimposition. He is Being, while the person having psychic powers is an individuality speaking to other individualities by means of tools of 'persuasion'.

Q. Can power be used simply out of vanity?

A. Yes. This is the less harmful of possibilities, even if the most fleeting. Vanity is one of the many psychological 'advantages' that one may receive from the exercise of a power.

Q. In short, are powers or faculties mere accidents of *prakṛti*?

A. Yes. By contrast *sat*, *cit*, *ānanda* are not attributes or accidents of Being, but are the *nature* of Being, consubstantial with Being itself.

Bliss or fulfilment is not a psychic power. Intelligence or Consciousness is not a psychic power but the faculty of sense perception, behind which there is the operation of Universal Intelligence, Being and Consciousness.

Power represents the exercise of a faculty which can come into being and die, exist and not exist. It operates, as we have already said, on the plane of duality and therefore on the plane of non-being. *Sat-*

cit-ānanda is Being, which is ever-existent since it belongs to non-becoming.

Power operates on the plane of *necessity*, while *sat-cit-ānanda* acts on the plane of *freedom*.

Material or psychic wealth is needed to acquire something that one does not possess; someone who possesses everything within himself does not seek either material or psychic wealth.

Q. Does the metaphysical pathway oppose such powers?

A. It cannot oppose them, as they are powers and faculties that belong to *prakṛti* itself. It cannot, obviously, agree with the use that is often made of them. Even Jesus made use of similar powers, and these were not only used wisely but we can say that they did not belong to the psychical sphere, as this sphere represents just a channel of the universal will. The universal Consciousness was making use of 'phenomena' for particular, and obviously non-individual, purposes.

RAPHAEL

Unity of Tradition

Raphael, having attained a synthesis of Knowledge (which is not associated with eclecticism or with syncretism), aims at 'presenting' the Universal Tradition in its many Eastern and Western expressions. He has spent a substantial number of years writing and publishing books on spiritual experience; his works include commentaries on the *Qabbālāh*, Hermeticism and Alchemy. He has also commented on and compared the Orphic Tradition with the works of Plato, Parmenides, and Plotinus. Furthermore, Raphael has written several books on the pathway of non-duality (*Advaita*). He has also translated and commented on a number of key Vedantic texts from the original Sanskrit.

With reference to Platonism, Raphael has highlighted the fact that, if we were to draw a parallel between Śaṅkara's *Advaita Vedānta* and a Traditional Western Philosophical Vision, we could refer to the Vision presented by Plato. Drawing such a parallel does not imply a search for reciprocal influences, but rather it points to something of paramount importance: a sole Truth, inherent in the doctrines (teachings) of several great thinkers who, although far apart in time and space, have reached similar and in some cases even identical conclusions.

One notices how Raphael's writings aim to manifest and underscore the Unity of Tradition from the metaphysical perspective. This does not mean that he is in opposition to a dualistic perspective, or to the various religious faiths, or 'points of view'.

An embodied real metaphysical Vision cannot be opposed to anything. What counts for Raphael is the unveiling, through living and being, which one has been able to contemplate.

In the light of the Unity of Tradition Raphael's writings or commentaries offer the intuition of the reader precise points of correspondence between Eastern and Western Teachings. These points of reference are useful for those who want to approach a comparative doctrinal study and to enter the spirit of the Unity of the Teaching.

For those who follow either the Eastern or the Western traditional line these correspondences help in comprehending how the *Philosophia Perennis* (Universal Tradition), which has no history and has not been formulated by human minds as such, 'comprehends universal truths that do not belong to any people or any age'. It is only for lack of 'comprehension' or 'synthetic vision' that one particular Branch is considered the only reliable one. From this position there can be only opposition and fanaticism. What degrades the Teaching is sentimental, fanatical devotionalism as well as proud intellectualism, which is critical and sterile, dogmatic and separative.

In Raphael's words: 'For those of us who aim at Realisation, our task is to get to the essence of every Teaching, because we know that, just as Truth is one, so Tradition is one even if, just like Truth, Tradition may be viewed from a plurality of apparently different points of view. We must abandon all disquisitions concerning the phenomenal process of becoming, and move onto the plane of Being. In other words, we must have a Philosophy of Being as the foundation of our search and of our realisation.'[1]

---

[1] See Raphael, *Tat tvam asi*, (That thou art). Aurea Vidyā, New York.

Raphael interprets spiritual practice as a 'Pathway of Fire'. Here is what he writes: 'The "Path of Fire" is the pathway which each disciple follows in all branches of the Tradition; it is the Way of Return. Therefore, it is not the particular teaching of an individual or the path parallel to the one and only Main Road... After all, every disciple follows his own "Path of Fire", no matter which Branch of the Tradition he belongs to'.

In Raphael's view, what is important is to express through living and being the truth that one has been able to contemplate. Thus, for each being, one's expression of thought and action must be coherent and in agreement with one's own specific *dharma*.

After more than 60 years of teaching, in both oral and written format, Raphael withdrew into *mahāsamādhi*.

* * *

May Raphael's Consciousness, an expression of Unity of Tradition, guide and illumine along this *Opus* all those who donate their *mens informalis* (formless mind) to the attainment of the highest known Realisation.

PUBLICATIONS

Aurea Vidyā Collection

1. Raphael, ***The Threefold Pathway of Fire***, Thoughts that Vibrate for an Alchemical, Æsthetical, and Metaphysical ascesis

Retail ISBN 978-1-931406-00-0
Amazon 978-1-931406-75-8
Apple etal. 978-1-931406-46-8 forthcoming

2. Raphael, ***At the Source of Life***, Questions and Answers concerning the Ultimate Reality

Retail ISBN 978-1-931406-01-7
Amazon 979-8-576124-75-6
Apple etal. 978-1-931406-32-1

3. Raphael, ***Beyond the illusion of the ego***, Synthesis of a Realizative Process

Retail ISBN 978-1-931406-03-1
Amazon 979-8-576629-52-7 forthcoming
Apple etal. 978-1-931406-18-5 forthcoming

4. Raphael, ***Tat tvam asi***, That thou art, The Path of Fire According to the Asparśavāda

Retail ISBN 978-1-931406-02-4
Amazon 979-8-583067-52-7 forthcoming
Apple etal. 978-1-931406-34-5

5. Gauḍapāda, ***Māṇḍūkyakārikā***, The Metaphysical Path of *Vedānta**

Retail ISBN 978-1-931406-04-8
Amazon 979-8-727363-30-0 forthcoming
Apple etal. 978-1-931406-45-1 forthcoming

6. Raphael, ***Orphism and the Initiatory Tradition***
Retail ISBN 978-1-931406-05-5
Amazon 979-8-539590-78-9
Apple etal. 978-1-931406-35-2

7. Śaṅkara, ***Ātmabodha***, Self-knowledge*
Retail ISBN 978-1-931406-06-2
Amazon 978-1-466492-56-1 forthcoming
Apple etal. 978-1-931406-53-6 forthcoming

8. Raphael, ***Initiation into the Philosophy of Plato***
Retail ISBN 978-1-931406-07-9
Amazon 978-1-466486-98-0
Apple etal. 978-1-931406-52-9

9. Śaṅkara, ***Vivekacūḍāmaṇi***, The Crest-jewel of Discernment*
Retail ISBN 978-1-931406-08-6
Amazon 978-1-931406-76-5
Apple etal. 978-1-931406-48-2 forthcoming

10. ***Dṛdṛśyaviveka***, A philosophical investigation into the nature of the 'Seer' and the 'seen'*
Retail ISBN 978-1-931406-09-3
Amazon 979-8-669178-69-7
Apple etal. 978-1-931406-28-4

11. Parmenides, ***On the Order of Nature***, Περί φύσεως, For a Philosophical Ascesis*
Retail ISBN 978-1-931406-10-9
Amazon 979-8-698821-95-3
Apple etal. 978-1-931406-22-2

12. Raphael, ***The Science of Love***, From the desire of the senses to the Intellect of Love
Retail ISBN 978-1-931406-12-3
Amazon 978-1-931406-12-3 forthcoming
Apple etal. 978-1-931406-54-3 forthcoming

13. Vyāsa, ***Bhagavadgītā***, The Celestial Song*
Retail ISBN 978-1-931406-13-0
Amazon 979-8-562809-02-5
Apple etal. 978-1-931406-50-5

14. Raphael, ***The Pathway of Fire according to the Qabbālāh*** (Ehjeh 'Ašer 'Ehjeh), I am That I am
Retail ISBN 978-1-931406-14-7
Amazon 978-1-931406-81-9 forthcoming
Apple etal. 978-1-931406-49-9 forthcoming

15. Patañjali, ***The Regal Way to Realization***, Yogadarśana*
Retail ISBN 978-1-931406-15-4
Amazon 978-1-931406-82-6 forthcoming
Apple etal. 978-1-931406-20-8

16. Raphael, ***Beyond Doubt***, Approaches to Non-duality
Retail ISBN 978-1-931406-16-1
Amazon 979-8-657281-16-3
Apple etal. 978-1-931406-25-3

17. Bādarāyaṇa, ***Brahmasūtra****
Retail ISBN 978-1-931406-17-8
Amazon 978-1-931406-83-3 forthcoming
Apple etal. 978-1-931406-47-5 forthcoming

18. Śaṅkara, ***Aparokṣānubhūti***, Self-realization*
Retail ISBN 978-1-931406-19-2
Amazon 979-8-664813-35-7 forthcoming
Apple etal. 978-1-931406-30-7

19. Raphael, ***The Pathway of Non-Duality***, Advaitavāda
Retail ISBN 978-1-931406-21-5
Amazon 979-8-552322-16-9
Apple etal. 978-1-931406-24-6

20. ***Five Upaniṣads***, Īśa, Kaivalya, Sarvasāra, Amṛtabindu, Atharvaśira*

Retail ISBN 978-1-931406-26-0
Amazon 978-1-707406-73-9
Apple etal. 978-1-931406-29-1

21. Raphael, ***The Philosophy of Being,*** A conception of life for coming out of the turmoil of individual and social conflict

Retail ISBN 978-1-931406-27-7
Amazon 979-8-630006-39-4
Apple etal. 978-1-931406-31-4

22. Raphael, ***Awakening***

Retail ISBN 978-1-931406-44-4
Amazon 979-8-716953-07-9
Apple etal. 978-1-931406-33-8

23. Raphael, ***Essence and Purpose of Yoga***, Initiatory ways to the Transcendent

Retail ISBN 978-1-931406-36-9
Amazon 978-1-931406-61-1
Apple etal. 978-1-931406-62-8

24. Śaṅkara, ***Short Works***, Treatises and Hymns*

Retail ISBN 978-1-931406-71-0
Amazon 978-1-931406-55-0
Apple etal. 978-1-931406-56-7

Related Publications

A brief biography, ***Śaṅkara***
Aurea Vidyā. New York.

Retail ISBN 978-1-931406-11-6
Amazon 978-1-931406-85-7 forthcoming

Forthcoming Publications

Māṇḍūkya Upaniṣad, with the Gauḍapāda's *kārikās* and the Commentary of Śaṅkara*

Retail ISBN 978-1-931406-37-6
Amazon 978-1-931406-57-4
Apple etal. 978-1-931406-58-1

Upaniṣads*

Retail ISBN 978-1-931406-38-3
Amazon 978-1-931406-59-8
Apple etal. 978-1-931406-60-4

Self-knowledge, The Harmonization of Psychic Energy. Edited by the Kevala Group

Retail ISBN 978-1-931406-40-6
Amazon 978-1-931406-63-5
Apple etal. 978-1-931406-64-2

Uttaragītā*

Retail ISBN 978-1-931406-68-0
Amazon 978-1-931406-69-7
Apple etal. 978-1-931406-70-3

Sanskrit Glossary

Retail ISBN 978-1-931406-67-3
Amazon 978-1-931406-65-9
Apple etal. 978-1-931406-66-6

* Translation from Sanskrit or Greek and Commentary by Raphael.

Aurea Vidyā is the Publishing House of the Parmenides Traditional Philosophy Foundation, a Not-for-Profit Organization whose purpose is to make Perennial Philosophy accessible.

The Foundation goes about its purpose in a number of ways: by publishing and distributing Traditional Philosophy texts with Aurea Vidyā, by offering individual and group encounters, by providing a Reading Room and daily Meditations, at its Center.

* * *

Those readers who have an interest in Traditional Philosophy are welcome to contact the Foundation at: parmenides.foundation@earthlink.net.

www.ingramcontent.com/pod-product-compliance
Lightning Source LLC
Chambersburg PA
CBHW032002080426
42735CB00007B/478
* 9 7 8 1 9 3 1 4 0 6 2 1 5 *